Shattered Lives

ENDORSEMENTS

"Malia Crandall's stirring memoir, *Shattered Lives: Why Women Stay*, was a startling eye-opener for me. Above and beyond details of the horrific abuse she endured for more than four decades was my realization that some behaviors I had considered acceptable or even normal were actually abusive. I also gained a comprehensive understanding of why women in abusive relationships either stay or keep returning to their abusers; while I had once judged them as weak or incapable, I now know the myriad of complex factors that make it so difficult for so many of them to escape even life-threatening situations. As a result of reading Malia's brave work and buoyed by the redemptive way her story ends, I feel empowered to understand and help those around me who may be suffering from any degree of abuse or harm. It's a story I won't soon forget, and I applaud her ability to relive and then share the things that would have literally broken so many."

—Kathryn Jenkins Oveson
Former board member, Utah County Mental Health Association

"*Shattered Lives: Why Women Stay* tells the heartbreaking real-life story that is almost too horrific to believe, which is probably why it took decades for her to remember where it all began at age four. Her experiences are vividly relived, revealing the ongoing abuse in her life, from her childhood all the way into adulthood. Malia's courage and strength to overcome abuse and tell her story is an inspiration to all."

—Ashley R.
Domestic Violence Advocate

SHATTERED LIVES

WHY WOMEN STAY

MALIA B. CRANDALL

NEW YORK

LONDON • NASHVILLE • MELBOURNE • VANCOUVER

SHATTERED LIVES

WHY WOMEN STAY

Published in New York, New York, by Morgan James Publishing. Morgan James is a trademark of Morgan James, LLC. www.MorganJamesPublishing.com

Proudly distributed by Ingram Publisher Services.

Morgan James BOGO™

A **FREE** ebook edition is available for you or a friend with the purchase of this print book.

_____

CLEARLY SIGN YOUR NAME ABOVE

Instructions to claim your free ebook edition:
1. Visit MorganJamesBOGO.com
2. Sign your name CLEARLY in the space above
3. Complete the form and submit a photo of this entire page
4. You or your friend can download the ebook to your preferred device

ISBN 9781631956256 paperback
ISBN 9781631956263 ebook
Library of Congress Control Number:
2021938191

Cover and Interior Design by:
Chris Treccani
www.3dogcreative.net

Morgan James PUBLISHING Builds with... Habitat for Humanity® Peninsula and Greater Williamsburg

Morgan James is a proud partner of Habitat for Humanity Peninsula and Greater Williamsburg. Partners in building since 2006.

Get involved today! Visit MorganJamesPublishing.com/giving-back

TABLE OF CONTENTS

ACKNOWLEDGMENTS

I would like to thank my husband, Scott, who repeatedly encouraged me to continue with this book when I got discouraged. He had faith in me when I had only doubt. We've been married more than eleven years. He is the love of my life, and he has taught me that there are actually good men in this world. I love him with all my heart.

I also want to thank my editor, Kathryn Jenkins Oveson, who helped make this book a reality by correcting my many errors caused by severe complex PTSD and its associated cognitive issues. She has been an angel, to say the least. She has put many hours into this and went above and beyond what anyone else would have done for me. Without her help, you would not be reading this now.

Thanks to Angie Fenimore, who runs the Calliope Writing Course. I found Angie and her course on Facebook. She pushed me and got me through some really rough times, giving me the confidence to pitch my story to editors—especially the one who accepted my story and thought what I had to say was of importance.

Thanks to all six of my children, one of whom is in heaven; I know I'll see him again. They have each taught me more than I could ever teach them. Being a mom is the best thing in the world, as long as you are a good one.

Lastly, thanks to my late mother, who always told me I wasn't good enough and that I couldn't do certain things. She caused me to push myself to my limits and do more than I otherwise could, including quitting smoking and writing this book. She has taught me that there really *is* a light at the end of the dark tunnel, because she was part of the darkness in my life, and now I can live in the sunlight. Because of her, I have tried harder, and instead of doubting myself, I am now confident that I *do* matter and can make a difference in this world—and that I actually have a purpose. I can still love myself even if she never loved me.

PREFACE

Although many of you may not agree with my spiritual or religious views, I am writing in the hope that the core concept of this book will resonate with those who are either in a domestic violence situation or know someone who is, whether it be a parent, friend, coworker, sibling, or neighbor.

I hope to broaden the horizon on "why women stay" and the complicated circle of abuse that surrounds it. Why you need to feel consistency and to feel safe, no matter how many times you have tried to get away. Why you need to always return to the familiar, facing what you know, as bad as it may be, rather than returning to the unknown.

Most of all, I want to let those who think women who stay are just crazy or confused know that this is just as much of a disease as alcoholism, heroin addiction, or any other addiction.

Only Divine intervention can help you turn things around—but know, above everything else, *there is hope.* There is light at the end of the tunnel—it is God, or whoever or whatever you deem to be a source of power greater than yourself.

There are so many sociopaths and men who manipulate and use mind control who are good at doing what they do; they can make you feel like you are at fault—that you are the crazy one for questioning their behavior. Even when you swore this was the very last time, you are left wondering how in the world it happened again. You are by no means crazy. It's much easier to leave than to stay away. You most likely have been brainwashed, and there is a certain amount of dis-association involved in most domestic violence cases.

We fail to see all the lies, we believe our abusers, and we cover up for them. Why? Because it is all we know. We believe we are the cause, and we are ashamed. *You can get out.* You can find real love and have a life full of peace and contentment even after doing the most bizarre things to maintain your forbidden secret from the rest of the world.

This book is dedicated to all women who have suffered and/or died at the hands of these cowardly beasts and to all those who are still suffering in hopelessness. In this country alone, three women are killed every day by their intimate partners. It could be a neighbor, a friend, a loved one, or even you.

Just remember—to thine own self be true! There is a scene in *Heat* in which Neil McCauley (Robert De Niro) says, "Allow nothing in your life that you cannot walk out on in thirty seconds flat." Being able to walk away means you won't ever get too attached to your belongings; being unattached to "stuff" makes your life tremendously flexible and filled with opportunity. It means you can look forward to dreams you never could have imagined coming true, dreams that for so long have seemed distant and vague and out of your reach. You can now embrace and live beyond your wildest dreams.

You can finally own up to who you really are—a queen who demands respect and love and deserves nothing less. You deserve the very best life has to offer, and Heavenly Father wants nothing less than your total joy and happiness in this life and the life beyond.

Set boundaries and stick to them and never allow anyone to disrespect you or abuse you in any way, shape, or form. If someone does, you can solve the problem by cutting him out of your life at any moment. You cannot change other people. You are the one who needs to decide to leave, as scary as that may be. Trusting God and moving forward is the only way to find true love, happiness, and joy, even if it means being alone. As you do, you will rise above being a victim and become a victor.

INTRODUCTION

I was so attached to my stuff that I couldn't leave without it; it was a part of me. So, I'd wait until my husband would be out of town for a few days—then I'd rent the largest U-Haul available, gather up some friends, and pack up every single thing that was mine or ours. I lived by the rule that what's yours is mine and what's mine is mine. I was very selfish and left little behind for my now ex-husband.

This got tiring with each move, so I eventually installed a trailer hitch to the back of my Tahoe and just took a small trailer of stuff. I was never willing to leave everything behind and start over; for me, that was never an option. If I planned well, I could always take what I wanted. Toward the very end, I took only my personal belongings.

I know in many cases, women with children barely escape with nothing but the clothes on their backs. You have to do what is best for you, and if getting out with nothing means you get to live, then that is worth it. After all, God knows your needs, and He will fill in the gaps with everything you need and more if you just put your trust in Him.

The Lord giveth, the Lord taketh away, and the Lord giveth more. You need to be willing to Let Go and Let God and fully trust Him when necessary.

Somehow those of us who are abused don't seek help for many reasons. We may think we are the cause. We might be too afraid to leave. Maybe money is an issue, and at least by staying, we have a roof over our heads and food to eat. We think over time our abuser will change. And on and on. . . .

But how do you think God—or the universe, or a Higher Power greater than you—views women in general, especially those who are abused? Does He want you to be disrespected, abused, even injured, and scared for your life every single day because you just don't know when your husband or significant other is going to snap again or when the next outburst of rage will be? You don't know what will set him off and to what degree he will explode, so you learn to walk on eggshells, always trying to please him and not rock the boat.

When Barbara Bartolome had her near-death experience (NDE), it was proof to me that God does not want women to be abused. I only wish I'd heard her experience many years earlier, as my religious beliefs caused me to feel that divorce was just wrong. It isn't—not always.

Barbara had an eight-year-old son and a five-month-old daughter, who is now a thirty-one-year-old nurse. Her husband said her NDE was a hallucination, so she didn't talk about it again for thirteen years. She is now the founder and director of the International Association of Near-Death Studies (IANDS) Santa Barbara. I am sharing part of her story with her permission, as she too was once an abused woman.

Her NDE talk was covered in a documentary by French film producer Anthony Chene, and it's available on YouTube at https://www.youtube.com/watch?v=zg3HnkSg38s. (If you enter *Barbara Bartolome NDE* in a search engine, you can access additional talks she has given.)

> I was so afraid of my ex-husband, so much so that I chose not to leave, for fear of what would happen to me and my children. I desperately hoped that I could do everything the way he liked it done, earn enough money to be worthy in his eyes, as well as meet all his expectations and every need or demand so that he would not be angered. I prayed that he would outgrow his angry outbursts, controlling and manipulative ways, and emotionally and physically abusive behaviors. I thought that I loved him; I forgave him for terrible outbursts and abuse that I never should have. I feared that if I left him, he might cut my car's brake lines or stage some accidental death because he would stand to receive a substantial amount of life insurance money.
>
> I had relocated more than 1,000 miles from my family and friends to marry him; he then openly and strongly discouraged my continued contact with them. His surly demeanor toward any of my longtime friends, if they came to visit me, or new people or work col-

leagues that I met and tried to build friendships with, had created a situation where I
was completely and profoundly unsupported.
I was afraid to disclose how bad it was to my
family or friends; mainly because I had been
previously married and divorced, I knew that
everyone would think poorly of me for making an even bigger mistake. I deeply knew
that I needed to leave him, but I didn't know
how it was possible to do it without having
him be outraged and dangerous, not only to
me but also to my young son from my previous marriage and to our daughter, who was
just a toddler at the time.

My 1987 NDE changed everything for
me, making me realize without any doubt that
I needed to find a safe way to permanently
exit his life. Up on that hospital ceiling, hovering above my lifeless body with the medical
team attempting to resuscitate me, I knew that
I could not leave my children's lives without causing massive damage to them by their
being left to be raised by their fathers . . . who
didn't want them and who had never shown
the capacity to be loving, kind, and supportive.
God, up on that hospital x-ray room ceiling
next to me, wanted me to evaluate my request
to be allowed to return to my children's lives
because I would also be returning to a dan-

gerous marriage. I was safe with Him, but I would not be safe if I chose to return to my life, because of my ex-husband's behaviors.

I was shown short film clips of abuse incidents that I had been subjected to, then God gave me all the time that I needed to evaluate the situation and decide to stay with Him, where I was safe, or return to my life for the sake of my children, where I would again be in a very dangerous marriage. By giving me the time, outside and above my body during my cardiac arrest, to evaluate all that I had done to try to alter, minimize, and eliminate my ex-husband's anger and abuse, I was able to conclude that nothing that I could do, or anything that the professionals that I had sought help from could do, would change my ex-husband's behavior. I realized, for the first time, that I needed to stop trying to change my ex-husband and, instead, change myself. I needed to get myself, and my children, safely out of the situation.

When I said, "If you let me go back [to my life], I promise that I will grow strong enough to leave him," I immediately lost my view of the medical team below me, and opened my eyes, in my body, and looked over the oxygen mask that had been placed on my face, into the face of the orthopedic surgeon who had just restarted my heart with a precordial thump. Twenty minutes later, when they had stabilized me and removed the oxygen mask from my face, I proceeded to tell the startled medical team every small detail that I had watched and listened to, while my body lay in cardiac arrest on the x-ray table below where my consciousness was above, on the ceiling.

After I left the hospital, I did strengthen myself and I began carefully planning my escape from the marriage. I had to be very patient until the right circumstances allowed me to move my children and me out of our home. The right time was when he was on a week-long business trip to Montreal, Quebec, Canada, and I obtained a judge's restraining order to protect us from my ex-husband's anger after he returned and discovered that we were gone. It was the beginning of a much better life for my children and me, but I had to be brave enough to launch it . . . because I never forgot that I had promised God I would get brave enough to do it. I'm so very happy that I experienced my NDE, and I'm so very thankful for all that it did to completely change the course of my life!

After leaving the meeting where I heard Barbara tell her story, I grabbed one of her cards so I could get in touch with her and share part of her story. It was and is a testimony to me that God wants only the best for all of His children, especially women, and that He holds us in high esteem. We share special talents and gifts that only women can, and above all, we have the highest calling in life—that of bearing children. We are His chosen daughters and have abilities beyond what we know. He would want us to be treated like the princesses and queens we truly are and have the potential to become.

Since Barbara confirmed there is a place we go to when we die, it only stands to reason there is a place we came from before birth. I believe it is from the presence of a loving Heavenly Father and Mother. Although we may not see it at the moment, or think it is fair, there is a purpose that will one day be made known to us. This life is like a school where we come to learn and make choices, good or bad—choices that will pave the way for us throughout eternity.

Again, these are *my* beliefs. God, grant me the serenity to accept the things I cannot change, the courage to change the things I can, and the wisdom to know the difference.

CHAPTER ONE

The day I was diagnosed with Post-Traumatic Stress Disorder (PTSD)—a debilitating mental-health condition triggered by a terrifying event—I was convinced it was the result of my seventeen-year abusive marriage.

I believed that for a long time. I now know that it goes back much further than that. Maybe—or most likely—generations back.

That's not an easy thing to grasp. One therapist maintained that some extremely traumatic event in my childhood terrified me. I remember telling him, "No, there was nothing like that in my childhood; it's all because of my abusive husband." That was easy for me to say at the time, because I didn't remember anything. He simply said that he didn't want to force it out of me and that one day I'd just remember it—or maybe I never would. I insisted that I was seeing him because I needed help getting out of an abusive relationship. (My husband at the time was clueless; he thought I was seeking therapy to work on myself.)

A subsequent counselor also tried to help me get out of my abusive marriage, and he couldn't hide his disappointment when I decided to stay with Brad. I asked if he'd be willing to do marriage counseling with us, but he refused, saying Brad "wasn't counseling material." Still, I stayed with Brad.

Then it happened.

I got lost on my way to work—a route I drove every day. I was confused and disoriented. I knew I needed serious help.

That's when Dr. O'Neal at Utah's Trauma Family Center diagnosed me with PTSD. He knew what he was talking about: he worked on-site following the attack on New York City's twin towers. He also had extensive experience helping veterans returning from war.

He too was convinced that something very traumatic happened to me in my childhood. He had me close my eyes and imagine I was a little girl; the adult version of me then comforted the child within, convincing me it wasn't my fault. After a few sessions, I was no longer jumping out of my skin every time someone walked downstairs and entered my bedroom.

His treatments normally took only five or six visits, so after that, I thought I was finished and stopped seeing him. I was fine for a time, but then it all came back. Something— almost always subconscious—triggered my memory, and I'd find myself being so disoriented behind the wheel that I wouldn't know where I was, even though I was somewhere I knew well. It was like being on a spinning wheel in a playground, hanging on for dear life as you get spun around and around until you're so dizzy, you're not quite sure where you are.

The day I got lost going to work I was listening to Kelly Clarkson's "The War Is Over." Part of the lyrics seemed to mirror my situation with Brad; in those lyrics, she is finally walking away—despite all efforts to pull her back—with the repeated sentiment, "You don't deserve me." I was certain the song reflected my situation with Brad. But years later, I realized that Dr. O'Neal might have been right.

It might not have been Brad. It might have been my mother.

Though I thought it was silly, I finally decided to ask my mom. She laughed it off, telling me that nothing traumatic ever happened to me when I was little.

But things didn't improve, and I soon figured out I had asked the wrong person. She was one of the perpetrators of what had happened, and once I started asking about it, she began to distance herself from me. She also managed to get my only brother to turn against me. Although we were never close, he now hates me and refers to me as his "late sister."

My Complex PTSD became so severe that I was approved for one year of disability. Kiara—a beautiful, petite woman with long, dark, curly hair—said I'd be re-evaluated after a year and could possibly qualify for three to five more years.

I was recently approved for seven more years.

One night I woke up, my head full of remembering things I wish I didn't have to know but needed to confront to heal. I grabbed my notebook and started to write.

So here I am, shaking after waking up in the middle of the night. Another day short-

ened by wanting to sleep to escape my reality, not even sure what it is/was. It's all beginning to make sense now, even though it seems to have no rhyme or reason at all—at least in my mind.

I have been diagnosed with fibromyalgia and chronic fatigue syndrome, and at times I just want to sleep for days. Sometimes I do. Even when I have important things to do, sleep prevails and overrides everything else, no matter the cost—just like my drinking did when I had to drink, no matter what.

Nothing matters but sleep, and I have to get there. Often, I can't fight it, no matter how hard I try. I have found myself falling asleep in the middle of doing lots of things, including driving. Thank goodness I had the where-withal to pull over; when I woke up, it was as if I was waking up from a bad drunk. Every-thing was spinning, and it took me a while to figure out where I was and how I had got-ten there. It seemed like my past was coming to the surface, yet my mind couldn't bear to know it, so it simply shut off to protect me.

CHAPTER TWO

I must have been about three years old.

My alcoholic father owed a huge tab at a local bar. I remember him once painting that bar to work off part of the money he owed.

I also remember often going over to the apartment of one of his "friends"; later I learned that friend was the owner of the bar. We called him "Boston Bob," and he had a big swimming pool and a couple of large dogs, one of which was a German shepherd. He was always happy to let us come over and swim.

As I walked through the apartment for the first time, I saw a collage of naked people hanging near the living room/kitchen. It was the first time I had ever seen a naked adult. Though I had no clue what was going on in the pictures, the people were having sex—some of them participating in orgies.

I was first taken to Boston Bob's when I was three, and I was told I couldn't be "used" until I was four. It was all my parents talked about—when I finally turned four, I could help them out financially. My mother could stop going to her church for help with bags of groceries. I would be four, and I would be special. It would be magical.

The day I turned four, I kept asking with excitement, "I'm four? I'm really four?" I just couldn't believe how lucky I was. There was something about that number that was magical—it was bringing something wonderful that was about to change in my life, or so I'd been told. I remember feeling special that day, like a princess wearing a crown and riding on a rainbow-colored unicorn.

Nothing could have been further from the truth.

The day I turned four, I was taken to Boston Bob's alone—without my brother. That's the day the sexual encounters began.

Whenever the sex started, I freaked out and started screaming. The German shepherd got right in my face, barking like crazy, and I was afraid he was going to eat me alive. I became so afraid I became paralyzed with fear, and I couldn't move a muscle.

It happened multiple times, often with multiple men.

One time, Boston Bob's girlfriend tried doing something very strange to me. I didn't understand what was going on, but I started squirming and tried to get her away from me.

The last time I was at Boston Bob's with my dad, I can still see my father walking away in shame after a deal they had made. Not so with my mother—she was more than happy to comply with whatever deal they made, since I was now a valued tool to help get my father out of debt. In her eyes, I was useless for anything else and a burden she never wanted to begin with.

After that, the abusers gave me a drink they called "coffee" before each session. The concoction—almost certainly alcohol or some kind of drug—sedated me almost to a point of sleep; nothing seemed to matter, and I didn't care what was going on because my head was too fuzzy to think. It also stopped me from fighting them off. They filmed each session and took lots of pictures as well. During those sessions, I felt I was outside of my own body. I now realize I was dissociating to protect myself and survive.

At home, I often poured water on my bed, pretending I had wet the bed because I was afraid to sleep there. My mom had to make me a bed on the couch instead.

I was taken to Boston Bob's until I was seven or eight. Other than once when I was in seventh grade, the last time I saw my dad I was in the second grade. Boston Bob's girlfriend had been making me a long dress; I wanted one so badly because all the girls in school were wearing them. One morning, my dad came home with the dress for me to try on. Before I knew it, my dad was on top of my mom on the bed, hitting her over and over in the face in what seemed like slow motion.

My dad left that day. I never got the dress—and I blamed myself for their separation, associating it with that long dress. In my mind, I never should have asked for the dress, and maybe my father would have stayed. As it turned out, I can't even count the number of times they split up and got back together again.

When he was around, my dad always had a beer—a Coors—in his hand, and at the time I thought that stuff had to be great! One day I stole one from the refrigerator, took it outside, popped the top, and took one sip. It looked so cool and bubbly, but it was the most disgusting stuff I had ever tasted. It tasted like a rancid poison you'd feed a rodent you were trying to exterminate. I poured the rest of it out. I was six.

I pretty much grew up without a dad in my life. I still remember the gift my father gave me for Christmas the year I turned four. Ironically, it was a stuffed German shepherd dog in a lying-down position. Despite my terrifying experiences at Boston Bob's, I loved that stuffed animal, and it never scared me like real dogs later would. I kept it until it was unrecognizable as more than a matted wad of rolled-up fur.

My mom always intimidated me; only five-foot-two, she had fiery red hair and an inner fire to match. She often got annoyed, blowing up amid profuse profanity. She had been a practicing Jehovah's Witness for thirteen years. I was too young to know what her religion stood for, but I knew the American flag was considered evil, as was saluting it. I also knew we couldn't celebrate any holidays. During school Christmas parties, we had to go in another room and sit with other Jehovah's Witnesses and wait for time to go by while doing practically nothing. I felt different from the rest of the world, and not in a good way. My mother's religion did teach me to pray, however. As a child, I had a connection with God and always prayed.

My mom may have been religious as far as her church was concerned, but her treatment of me was anything but. She called me an "ugly little creep"—a label that stuck in my head. Not once as a child do I remember my mother telling me I was pretty or that I was loved. (Much later, when my brother was away in the Air Force, she did express love for me; at that time, I was all she had.)

From as early as I can remember, I never felt good enough. In school, girls went into the bathroom and combed their hair; if I ever looked in the mirror to primp myself, I stopped abruptly, thinking the other girls wondered why I was even bothering. I figured I was just wasting my time because I was ugly, and nothing I could do would improve my looks.

Over the years my mother called me names, verbally abusing me by calling me a fat pig (though I was never overweight), a stupid little kid, or an ugly creep. While I was growing up, I truly believed I was fat, ugly, and stupid. As I got older, college was never an option because I believed I was stupid. Why would a stupid person even try?

Being called a "fat pig" led to an eating disorder. I began with anorexia; when I could no longer starve myself, I'd eat but then feel so guilty I'd get rid of it so I wouldn't gain weight. Eventually, it became a coping mechanism, and I binged on huge amounts of food. Eventually, I went numb, and all my problems seemed distant and faded away for a while. Sometimes I counted calories religiously; other times, I'd give up and binge and purge—sometimes repeatedly, until I was exhausted. My behavior was more like a drug that helped me temporarily escape from all my problems. To this day, I feel more comfortable being underweight. If I'm at a healthy weight, I feel fat.

My mom took me and my brother, Jim—a husky blonde with buck teeth—on several trips to southern California to visit her mother. I heard my mom telling her how I had saved their finances and what I was being used for. I also heard her tell my grandmother that she never wanted me—she wanted only one child, a boy, and she had my brother. She said she had me only in an attempt to get my father to stop running around chasing other women and going out drinking all night, but it hadn't changed anything.

Once when my parents were separated, my grandmother—who also had short, red hair—came to live with us. I never knew why she didn't like me. She always gave me the evil eye and pointed her finger at me mockingly as if to tell me what a bad little girl I was. She used to always give me "that" look and scold me.

My grandmother was supposed to babysit us while Mom went to work, but she ignored us and simply did her own thing, whatever that was. Once when she was busy with something else, my friend and I went out on the busy street. We had seen men hitchhiking but thought they were merely using their thumbs to let everyone know which way to go. So, we stuck our thumbs out, pointing in the direction of the busy traffic from our side of the street. Before long, a man in a very nice, shiny car pulled over; he was almost as black as his car, and he invited us to get in. Thankfully, our fear made us run instead.

Another time, Jim and I went out to play behind the house. It had rained a lot, and we had gotten very dirty. When my mother got home, she was furious, and she lectured my grandmother.

That's when the terror began.

My grandmother allowed Jim to go outside, but she put me in a clothes hamper and turned it upside down; I had no way of getting out. I was horrified every time she got the hamper out because I knew what she was going to do. I hated being in that cramped, dark space; the musty smell of dirty clothes and lack of air made it as hot as an oven. I usually ended up falling asleep and often wet my pants, which my mother scolded me for as soon as she got home. I also got scratches on my arms and legs from the inside of the wicker basket.

Dr. O'Neal told me recently that if my grandmother were capable of all that, just imagine what else she could have done. He maintained that I was probably just skimming the surface as far as my memories about her were concerned. Mercifully, my grandmother's time in our house was short-lived, as my parents got back together for the last time not long after that.

I remember being taken to the doctor only once. Jim and I both had severe ringworm, and we were not allowed back in school until it was taken care of. Back then, they plucked the hair around each ringworm on the scalp, applied medicine, and covered our heads with a cap so we could go to school. Later I was allowed to wear a scarf.

Every year, my entire wardrobe came from a huge thrift store. It seemed like we drove for hours to get there, and we spent the entire day shopping. Jim never got anything from there; I was told that since he wore a husky size, his clothes had to be bought brand new. To this day, I shy away from thrift shops.

My brother is two and a half years to the day older than I am and was always pampered and spoiled. He was her favored "golden child" until the day she died, October 17, 2017. As just one example, I remember once going to the Arboretum in Arcadia, California. It was a beautiful place with botanical flowers, a historic home, and even quicksand covered with rope-like mats. There was a waterfall and a huge, towering fountain; we were even able to see bees making honey. On the tour bus, we got a good whiff of the popcorn tree, which smelled so much like the real thing.

When my mom took us into the gift shop, of course, we both wanted toys or something else to bring home. Mom told me that Jim was the only one who could have something because he was older—and if he made a scene crying, it would be a lot more embarrassing than if I cried. He got an expensive item; I got one of the cheapest items, a California orange made out of a soft material filled with air. In my mind, the message was clear: he was more valued, more loved.

That wasn't the only evidence of favoritism. Jim always got what he wanted when my mother could afford it. For example, he got a minibike that I wasn't allowed to touch; he also got a BB gun and all kinds of other things.

I remember getting only two dolls in my entire life. One was called a "flatsy doll"; it had hair and was bendable like a Gumby toy. I also got a beautiful doll by saving up enough coupons on bottles of Breck shampoo. A few times I got paper dolls. Other than that, I never had any other dolls to play with, so I played with my brother's cars and army men when he'd allow it.

I also went across the alleyway to a friend's house. She had lots of Barbie dolls and all the accessories to go with them, and she let me play with them. I wanted a Barbie doll of my own so badly. But even though Jim got pretty much whatever he wanted, my mom told me a Barbie doll was just too expensive.

Jim was always doing something wrong or bad; if my mom found out, he always blamed it on me, and she always believed him. As long as I was around to blame and punish, he was never held accountable for his behavior. She had us take baths together, claiming it was faster to bathe two than one at a time. That went on until he was about ten and I was eight. By that time, he started wearing his underwear in the tub. Once he pooped in the tub and told Mom I did it, and I was the one who got in trouble for it.

Mom was devoted to the Jehovah's Witness religion, so my dad—who wasn't religious at all—was the one who bought me and Jim presents one Christmas. As much as I enjoyed receiving these gifts from my father, I have to admit I felt a tinge of guilt as well, since my mom taught us it was wrong. Other than the Christmas gifts that once, when I was four, he gave me presents only for a birthday or two.

On my eighth birthday, I received a birthday present in the mail from my grandmother. I was so excited by surprises—I knew she despised me, and with the arrival of the gift, I thought maybe things had finally changed. Then I opened the present. It was one of those push toys babies use when they are just learning how to walk; the eyes on it rolled while little colored balls inside popped as it was pushed around. The box read *Ages 2 and up*. It felt like a slap in the face.

I never saw my grandmother again after I turned eleven and we moved to Redding, California. However, I did inherit her evil stare. I'd later gaze at my children with that same look when I was angry, and they knew to watch it if I ever had that glare on my face. Even after her death, it was known at our house as "The Grandma Look."

I stopped seeing Dr. O'Neal not long after I started remembering details from my early childhood. Everything came flooding to the surface, and I was stunned. While I knew it had all happened, it was almost like a bad dream. I didn't want to know if there was more, so I canceled my future appointments with Dr. O'Neal; the mind can only take in so much at a time. Though he was a kind, fatherly person, I didn't want him to know my deepest, darkest secrets, and I didn't want more details of them flooding my already over-whelmed mind.

Even without the visits to Dr. O'Neal, I continued to remember incidents from my childhood. At first, I refused to believe some of them, perhaps out of a desire to protect my parents by covering up or minimizing their bad behavior.

But that only works for so long.

When I was in the seventh grade, Jim and I flew from California to Texas to visit my dad and his new wife, Lori. One of my three stepsisters was with me when my dad came home totally drunk and ferociously angry. He took off his belt and was ready to beat us but stopped. I still don't know what made him so angry.

When we had visited my dad and Lori in California, they had plenty of food and cookies and all kinds of good things to eat. As we arrived in Texas, though, my stepsister confessed that the array of food in California had been nothing more than a plot to impress us. That night, we had only one can of green beans for dinner because there was absolutely nothing left in the house—my dad and Lori were at the bars when they weren't working. I hated green beans for many years after that.

Mom wasn't much into cooking. She was big on opening cans of vegetable soup and cooking TV dinners with beans, rice, and cheese enchiladas. After a while, she simply stopped cooking, and we never sat together during dinner. Though I never liked meat, I slowly began eating things with ground beef in them. (I've since become a vegetarian.)

My mother didn't seem concerned about any illnesses or injuries I had. Not too long ago, my dermatologist asked me how I got the big scar on my back. When I laughed at him, he said, "I'm serious." He positioned a mirror to show me a two-inch scar on my back and told me the scar was very old. I still have no idea how or when I got the scar. I jokingly told the dermatologist I was stabbed in the back—but I get chills when I realize how true that could be.

Once I got poison oak so severe that my eyes were swollen and the skin around my mouth was covered with scabs. I could barely open my mouth to eat and didn't even recognize myself when I looked in the mirror. But my brother was fine, so I was never taken to see a doctor.

When I was in the eighth grade, I met Jackie, a thin, pretty blonde who had moved from Stockton. One day I was driving Jackie's motorcycle. I had no clue what I was doing, and when I approached the corner, I turned the handles as I would have done on a bicycle. I skidded sideways onto the road, sustaining a major muffler burn on my right leg and a serious wound on my left knee, which was embedded with rocks and gravel. Though anyone else would have been taken to an urgent care facility or an emergency room, my mom just took me home and told me to take a bath.

My mother's lack of support extended beyond health concerns. I was never supported in school in any way, and it didn't even matter to my mom what my grades were, so I averaged a *C* in most classes. My mom also failed to go to my eighth-grade graduation. For the graduation, I had to borrow an ugly dress from my aunt Barbara because I didn't have anything else. All I remember is that the dress was blue and looked very outdated compared to the dresses all the other girls wore.

CHAPTER THREE

By the time I was in third grade, I developed obses-sive-compulsive disorder (OCD), and I had a problem with touching certain textures. If I touched something with one finger, I had to touch it with the opposite finger. If I touched it more than once, it had to equal four times, then in multiples of four—maybe because I still thought four was my magical number. I had to do this touching routine when I sat at my desk in school, which meant I had to try to hide it so others wouldn't know what I was doing. *I* didn't know what I was doing. I just knew I had to do it to maintain some sense of identity and control over my life; it made me feel safe and secure.

I also had severe abandonment issues and terrible sepa-ration anxiety. If I encountered a pole whose cable extended to the ground, I had to walk around it. If I went through it, I felt I was separating myself from everyone—especially my mom, who I felt I needed. I feared that going through some-thing like that might lead me into another dimension, place, or time away from my mother forever.

When I got to fourth grade, no one in my class knew me, so I started saluting the flag like everyone else. I just wanted so badly to fit in. Then I found out another boy in my class was a Jehovah's Witness, so I had to comply with the church's standards.

That was also the year I tried out for a talent show with my best friend, Lisa. She made up a dance to a song called "War." Quite by coincidence, we wore matching checkered dresses— hers was blue and white, and mine was red and white. I hated being in the spotlight, having people judge me. I felt I had already been judged enough to last a lifetime. After the audition, a boy in my class told me I didn't know how to dance. I had never felt so humiliated and embarrassed, and I grew up afraid to even try to dance.

We were often shipped off to different babysitters, which might be why I always felt abandoned; my mom made me cheese sandwiches with mayo and mustard for breakfast before dropping me off at a sitter's house. There were so many sitters, and I remember my mom talking about how hard it was to find a good one.

One of my sitters was a woman who owned horses. However, she was babysitting far too many kids, so she often made several of us go inside so she wouldn't get caught. While at her home, I once saw a man over the fence sitting in his car with his pants pulled down, masturbating. I wasn't quite sure what he was doing but knew it made me very uncomfortable. We eventually left that sitter because she beat us all with a belt. I had a bruise on my thumb because my hands were covering my butt—but we left that sitter for my brother's sake.

In southern California schools, the dress code dictated that girls could wear pants only when it rained. Since it rained so rarely, I didn't even own a pair of pants. But by the time we got settled in and I started going to my new school, I discovered that all the girls there wore pants; only rarely did one wear a dress. Once again, I didn't fit in.

My mom soon got a job at an electrical assembly line making parts for eye doctors to wear on the tips of their fingers. My uncle David, who lived with us by then, worked for the mosquito abatement company. We had inflatable furniture in the first duplex where we lived. We had gotten three little puppies, and one day they somehow got from the backyard to inside the house. There went the inflatable furniture; they tore the house apart. There went the puppies, too; they were given away.

I had a friend named Julie who lived around the corner. She was short, a bit overweight, and had slightly buck teeth, though she was a pretty girl. Julie and I got our first job across the street from her house. A woman who had an office there gave us a dime for doing chores like dusting, running the cordless vacuum, and so on. We immediately went to the corner store and each bought a huge, multicolored lollipop for a dime. We soon started working for a dealer who sold Lowry pianos and organs next to the office where we had been working. We dusted all the pianos and organs, and we each got paid a dollar. One day we went in the front door, only to find that no one else was in the store. We eventually called the police—the owner had forgotten to lock the door.

The year I was eleven, my mom became good friends with one of the women she worked with who had a daughter my age named Karen; we soon became best friends. This woman and her daughters stole a lot of merchandise, and one day they took me and my mom and taught us how to steal. Shoplifting was so easy back then; there were no security tags on the clothes, and you could take an unlimited number of items into the fitting rooms. The first time we went I was afraid, but after putting a few items in my purse and getting away with it, I was thrilled. To have my mother's permission made it all the better.

I went from only a few second-hand clothes to having whatever clothes I wanted; by the time I was in the sixth grade, I had a whole new wardrobe. One summer I remember having fourteen bikinis. I felt I could have any clothes I wanted, and I finally felt as good as everyone else. It was especially great having my mom's blessing—she didn't care if I stole my wardrobe because at least it was no money out of her pocket.

Even though I had great clothes, I still didn't fit in because of the occasional sleepover I was allowed to have. It was hard to explain to my friends that I had one room, my brother had another, and the one with the lock on the door belonged to my mom and my uncle. Everyone knew what was going on. It was incest, plain and simple, yet nobody talked about it. It was the forbidden secret—the can of worms no one wanted to open.

While it doesn't excuse the incest, my mother and my uncle grew up in severe dysfunction. My grandmother had ten kids; my mom was the oldest. My alcoholic grandfather moved from one place to another, and my grandmother finally got tired of it, so she settled in Hanford, California. She could no longer afford to care for all her children financially, so she decided to keep the first three—the ones with whom she had bonded—and she gave the rest up for adoption.

That didn't stop her from having more children with other men. Her method of birth control was simple: get pregnant, have an unwanted child, give it away. One of them died along the way. The last was a set of twins, Barbara and David. I'm certain the unstable family situation was a hardship for my mom, but somewhere along the way she became an evil person who later treated me terribly.

My twin aunt and uncle, Barbara and David, didn't find out they were adopted until they were seventeen; and at that point, they contacted my mom. Soon after that my uncle David came to live with us. We completely stopped going to church, and he talked Mom into moving from southern California to northern California. We moved to Redding when I was in the fifth grade.

My dad came by one day and saw a picture of a young, attractive man standing by his motorcycle; my mom had framed it, and it was displayed on an end table in our living room. Dad picked it up, looked at it a while, then asked, "Who's this?"

My mom feigned innocence as she said, "My brother."

But there was nothing innocent about it.

Karen and I continued our theft, moving on from mere clothing. We stole bedspreads from the local hotels when the maids were cleaning the rooms. One day we stole a juice machine from the Holiday Inn. The plan was for my brother to open it, and we'd split the change three ways. As fate would have it, they had just filled the machine. We each got a quarter and had lots of juice in the refrigerator. On another occasion, it was my job to sneak up and grab a ten-speed bike from in front of a house; my brother shoved it in the trunk of the car, and my mom was the getaway driver. My mom once got caught stealing aquarium sealant.

Another time Karen and I got caught stealing, and they called my mom. I was terrified—more afraid of her than of being caught stealing. She arrived at the store raging with anger, and she proceeded to scream and yell at us in the store. We rode our bikes home, and when we got there, she just laughed the whole thing off. To her, it was nothing more than funny.

Eventually, my mom and brother got caught stealing. My brother took the blame for stealing a police car radio, all the bikes, and the bike parts—including the bike and the juice machine I stole. I always thought he was being nice to cover for me, but I recently realized it was probably more so that my mom wouldn't get implicated as being the getaway driver. My brother went to juvenile lockup for a time, and my mom went to jail on weekends. The *Redding Record Searchlight* ran a story on them headlined, "Mother/Son Team."

It became too embarrassing for me to be home—especially after a police paddy wagon parked in the driveway and cops went through everything in our home, doing things like taking the backs off television sets to get the serial numbers. I decided it was better to stay away as much as I could, so I did. You'd think a mother would question a twelve-year-old girl for always being gone, but I later discovered that she liked it better when I wasn't around. I was no longer in her way, and since my brother was also away partying with friends, she was free to openly show her love for my uncle.

I had no patience and a very short temper at that time in my life. One day my brother made me so mad that I threw a butter knife at his head; the butt end of the knife hit him in the ear. One day I was cooking bacon and couldn't get it to flip over right; I stirred it all up in the pan before dumping it all on the floor. Once I got so angry at my mom that I scratched both my arms as hard as I could, leaving marks. My aunt Barbara asked me why I scratched my arms, but I avoided answering. A guy I knew at school said I had "cat scratch fever," playing off the title of a popular song at the time.

Kristine, my best friend at the time, lived in my neighborhood. She introduced me to alcohol, cigarettes, and boys. She had long, reddish hair and large breasts for her age, so she attracted a lot of older boys.

Other than my sip of Coors when I was six, I had my first drink at age twelve. This time it was vodka and lemonade; I got black-out drunk and repeatedly told one of the drug dealers that I loved him. Then I fell, hitting my head on a glass terrarium and breaking it. I couldn't stop crying, insisting I had glass in my eyes. (Luckily, I didn't.) I managed to walk home—a short trip that in my condition seemed like miles—and then threw up all over the house.

My mom came home shortly afterward and asked me if I was sick. I told her I was just drunk, and she told me to go to bed. I had a horrible hangover for three days; I had never felt so sick. You'd think that would be enough to make me stop drinking, but every weekend I was back out with my friends, drinking and smoking cigarettes and pot at the age of twelve. (A liquor store in the neighborhood allowed me to buy my own cigarettes; back then, they were thirty-five cents a pack.) I had finally found a crowd I could actually fit in with. They didn't care if I was rich or poor, wore dresses or pants, or what religion I was; they just accepted me because I was one of them—a drinker and a user.

I drank the alcohol not for taste, but for the effect. It made me feel all the things my mother told me I wasn't—smart, pretty, and thin. I no longer felt that all other girls were a competitive threat; I was an equal, and I fit in.

One time my mom and uncle, who weren't regular drinkers, came home drunk from my mom's office Christmas party. My uncle couldn't stop laughing. He wrestled me to the ground, then grabbed the bottoms of my pants and started pulling them off. My mom just stood there watching, laughing but not saying a word. I twisted out of his grip and pulled my pants up before running away from them, not knowing what he might otherwise have done.

During this time, my mother paid Karen to steal my school clothes for the year. I wore whatever she picked out, but I liked almost everything she chose. Besides that, they were brand new.

But then I really blew it. My friend and I tried to make our hair lighter with a product called "Lemon Go Lightly"; instead of simply lightening, it turned my hair bright orange. My mom's friend told me to pour peroxide over it; I did, but it only got worse. My mom never offered to take me somewhere to get it fixed, and I never knew it was even an option to fix it, so I went through the entire eighth grade with bright-orange hair until it grew out. With both my mom and grandmother having red hair, the last thing I wanted was hair that even resembled red. I absolutely hated it.

CHAPTER FOUR

When I was almost thirteen, we moved from Redding to Anderson, California, settling on some property my uncle David's adoptive parents owned. The move didn't make things any better at home. I was awakened very early in the morning by having my hair pulled, being slapped in the face, and being called a fat pig, just because I did something like leaving a few dishes in the sink.

While living in Anderson, my mom and uncle David tried to make it look like they were just brother and sister—good friends. Yet everyone had their suspicions. By the time I was almost fifteen, my uncle got a woman from work pregnant; my mom was furious. I remember her saying to him, "You can get your balls from someone else from now on." Her vernacular was confused, but I think she meant he could get his sex elsewhere.

Not long after that, my mom and I moved into some low-income apartments by the Sacramento River in Anderson. I always seemed to have a sixth sense about things; I told one of my best friends that we were moving into those apartments before I was even told. That's where I lived while

I went to high school. My brother had already left home and joined the Air Force.

When I was a freshman in high school and not drinking too much, I met my first love, Mike; I was just fourteen years old. We met just passing by in the hall every day in between classes, and we had a mutual interest in each other. He was tall, thin, and handsome with long, wavy, brown hair. Karen's boyfriend Craig worked at the UA Cinema 3, and she helped Mike get a job there through Craig.

I was so in love with Mike. After we had been a couple for five months—my longest relationship up to that time—he broke up with me for one of the girls who had worked at the theater. I was crushed. That night, we had invited Mike over for dinner. We went to the park, where he broke up with me, and by the time we got home, my mom and David had already eaten; she was never one to make a big to-do about anything. So, he and I ate alone as I struggled not to fall apart.

At the age of fifteen, I started out becoming a weekend drinker; before long, I was drinking a day or so in between weekends, and finally, I became a daily drinker. I had crossed the line; I no longer had a choice but *had to* drink, no matter what. My drink of choice was Schlitz Stout Malt Liquor in the tall, sixteen-ounce cans, as I heard it got you drunker. I also drank it at room temperature because I was also told warm beer gets you drunker. Finally, I drank it through a straw because I heard that helped get you drunker. If I had been told standing naked on your head drinking warm beer through a straw got you even drunker, I'm sure I would have tried that too. I learned not to eat too much before going to parties as it took more to get drunk on a full stomach; I also avoided eating later on, because it sobered me up more quickly. As a result, I did a lot of drinking but not a lot of eating.

By then I had gotten caught smoking for the third time (I should mention I had my mom's permission), so I got kicked out of Anderson High School and enrolled at North Valley, the continuation school. Classes there were only three hours a day, which gave me more time to drink. The friends I partied with all started saying that I might be an alcoholic and might need help. How I resented them! After all, they were the friends I partied with; how dare they!

I knew my dad was an alcoholic. When I first realized how much he drank, I didn't know what an alcoholic was. When I finally asked someone, I was told that an alcoholic is a person who drinks every day. So, at the age of fifteen, I tried as hard as I could every single day not to drink; I kept track on the calendar hanging above my bed. One month I had four full days that I didn't drink, and I decided then and there that I wasn't an alcoholic.

After that, I quit worrying about it and just continued to live the lifestyle I had chosen—one that I thought would block out all the pain from my past but that inevitably caused me more pain and suffering. I had chosen alcohol to escape. My brother had chosen the Air Force to escape. Later I learned he had also chosen alcohol along with the Air Force.

I got pregnant at fifteen during a one-night stand with a guy named Mason. I used to cut school with some friends of mine, and we hung out at a bar where the bartender allowed us to play pool and listen to the jukebox. I met Mason at that bar; he was there from Oregon with two other friends. He did call for a second date, but I wasn't interested. When I told my mom I was pregnant, she was furious—and when I brought up the possibility of abortion, she supported the idea 110 percent. Mason never did find out he had gotten me pregnant.

My high-school friend Lucy and I used to drink all the time. She was half Indian, and her full-Indian mother had been institutionalized due to alcoholism. Lucy had her own place.

I was with Lucy when I met my second love, Walt.

Lucy and I had my mom buy us a bottle of brandy then drop us off at Redding Mall, knowing full well we were heading to Redding Park after we ate to party. The road through the park was in the shape of a figure eight, making it possible to cruise continuously; there was no closing time and no alcohol rules. (Later they made it more family-friendly, installing playground equipment for the kids, banning alcohol, and closing at nine p.m.)

Lucy and I were drunk and were yelling at cars as they drove by. Walt and his best friend stopped and asked us if we wanted to go cruising with them. I still remember that he wore a green sweatshirt with the sleeves cut off and had an afro because his brown hair was so curly. Walt was a bigger guy, and I felt tingly all over. It was love at first sight. We just continued to talk and/or see each other every single day.

Whenever Walt picked me up, he always wore a smile. Outside of being drunk and us fighting, he was a wonderful boyfriend who bought me clothes, gave me a really nice watch (that I still have), and took me to the fair and so many other places. This fat, stupid, ugly little girl actually had a real boyfriend—something I never thought I'd have—and I loved him to pieces. He had a nice turquoise charger with a wing on the back, and he had a good-paying job driving a front-end loader for the garbage company. He didn't smoke pot or cigarettes but didn't seem to mind that I did. Everything seemed magical, at least when we were sober. I don't think I ever truly felt loved by anyone until Walt came along, and it was an indescribable feeling. I was fifteen and he was nineteen.

Walt had just gotten a girl pregnant, and she kept the baby. I knew her from high school, and she ended up at the continuation school where I went. Eventually, he drove past the continuation school and I was able to sneak a photo of his baby out to him so he could at least see what his daughter looked like. The girl never asked for anything from him, and I'm not sure he ever met his daughter.

It was while I was dating Walt that I discovered bulimia. My mom brought me breakfast in bed, and I was starting to gain weight. One day the eggs and toast made me so sick that I threw up. That's when I thought, *This would be a good way to lose weight.* I thought I was the only one in the world doing such a thing, and I had no idea it even had a name.

I was always terrified that since Walt was a garbage man, he'd find my bags full of empty Schlitz Malt Liquor cans and would figure out just how much I drank. My drinking had become a real problem. I sometimes woke up in sordid places with people I didn't know and with no idea how I had gotten there; I often lost my shoes and purse. On those occasions, I went outside, looked around, and guessed which way to start hitchhiking home. Luckily, I always made it.

Once I was hitchhiking home around 6:30 a.m. The guy who picked me up stopped at a convenience store and asked if I wanted anything to drink. I had no idea there was anything other than alcohol to drink, so I asked for a sixteen-ounce Schlitz Malt Liquor; he got himself some coffee. I can just imagine now what he thought of me, but at the time I didn't really care. Besides, I didn't think my behavior was all that unusual. After all, everyone drank beer in the morning, right?

Walt and I were together for about fifteen months. We did everything together, and he was the love of my life. I thought we'd be together forever. We went to the lake, we went fishing, we went hunting, and so much more—but everything we did included alcohol. We did get engaged at one time, but Walt broke it off. When he broke up with me for good, I stole his best friend Brock, who drank himself into oblivion each day. Seven years later I learned that Walt broke up with me because of my drinking; even though Walt drank too, he didn't drink nearly as much as I did.

Brock and I hung out and drank a lot after that. He was a scrawny little guy who had itchy skin on his arms, and he often covered it up with women's face makeup. He never questioned how much I drank because we both drank way too much, so he didn't even notice. Once when we were together, he got pulled over by the police for drunk driving, and they took him to jail. When I asked what I was supposed to do, the officer gave me a dime to make a phone call. I called my mom. I was in Redding and we were living in Anderson, and she wasn't about to come and get me. I stood on the freeway onramp and started to hitchhike and got a ride practically to my door. I got lucky once again.

My drinking did occasionally cause me some real problems. Lucy and I once met a couple of guys at the park; we invited them to Lucy's place and were playing a board game when the guy I liked got mad at me and left. I had my mom's Ford Mustang, and I went after him only to drive into a ditch parallel to the railroad tracks. We thought we heard a train coming, so the first thing we did was try to push the car back up the hill. Then we ran from house to house, knocking on doors until someone answered. We asked them to call the cops. Turns out that track was no longer being used, and for some reason, I was not arrested, nor did I get a ticket, even though I was pretty drunk. As it was, I put a hole in the radiator and ruined a very nice car.

Another time, I had to do some community service after being arrested for having an open container at Redding Park. We had to use shovels and pull weeds; within minutes I had blisters because I didn't wear gloves. I called my mom, and she paid the $50 fine so I didn't have to work it off. I told the people there I was leaving because I was sick. I was truly grateful and surprised that my mother paid the fine for me because I was such a wimp; I never could have made it through the day.

When I was seventeen, Walt and I got back together for a short time; we lived at home with my mom, and I got pregnant with Walt. I really wanted to keep this baby so I would have a part of Walt, but I knew my mother would go crazy. Plus, I had done way too much drinking and feared the baby would be severely messed up. Since Walt didn't care what I did, I had another abortion. Because I was just past the third trimester, I had to go to Chico for the abortion. Distorted by the alcohol, it all seemed so surreal. I was just a child myself and didn't feel like I had a live child growing inside of me. I just didn't fully understand what I was doing. (That's ironic, considering I am pro-life now.)

Walt was my best friend and was always there for me. Even though he was a pretty good-sized guy, I was never afraid of him (even though, as I'll discuss, I should have been). Although my mom was no longer with my uncle David, she never set any kind of rules or boundaries for me whatsoever. Walt and I often went to Eureka for the weekend, a three-hour-plus drive, and my mom never said a word. She even allowed us to go to Disneyland for three days, and it was a twelve-hour drive each way.

When we broke up the second time, I took the breakup hard, even though I should have been the one to leave him. When we drank, he often gave me black eyes, bloody noses, and fat lips; he also broke my nose, finger, and jaw. I always had an excuse to explain away an injury, but I'm sure my mom must have known.

One time, Walt broke my jaw. We were standing on the sidewalk arguing, and he started punching himself in the face. I grabbed one of his arms to get him to stop, and he punched me with his free arm. I told the guys in the hospital emergency room that we were messing around with a football and someone's knee had hit me in the chin. My mouth got wired shut, so I could have nothing other than liquids.

Once Walt ordered pizza at a drive-in theater. He showed no remorse and thought it was kind of funny that he got to eat pizza while all I could do was drink Ensure or whatever other concoctions I could whip up in a blender. (I never did get an apology for the broken jaw until seven years later; even then he said, "It wasn't *that* bad; at least I never thrashed you around or anything.")

Actually, he *did* "thrash me around." I remember being at his friend's apartment when he started yelling at me, then held me by the throat over the second-story railing and knocked me to the ground before lifting me by my hair and throwing me into the apartment. A neighbor saw what was happening and called the cops. They arrived as we were leaving in Walt's car. They said they couldn't do anything to him unless I pressed charges. I did everything I could to assure them I was okay and to protect Walt from getting into any kind of trouble.

I loved him even after he abused me.

CHAPTER FIVE

still have nightmares about Gary, my mom's first real boy-friend.

Once she split from my dad, my mom didn't really date. She assumed *he* had gone to Mexico and gotten a cheap divorce; he assumed *she* had gotten a divorce. They lived as divorcees though they remained legally married until death. My dad remarried once; my mom remarried three times.

With that bizarre history, Gary was the first man my mom "dated"—and their relationship came about in an even more bizarre way. While working on an assembly line in Califor-nia, my mom began writing to Gary, who was in prison in Alabama; he was incarcerated there with the brother of one of Mom's coworkers.

Even though I was still a teenager, my mom got me to write to several random inmates in Alabama. We didn't even know why they were in prison.

After Mom wrote Gary for several months, he was released, and he boarded a Greyhound bus to come and live with us. He had deep lines in his face and was missing sev-eral teeth (he later got dentures). I was drinking a lot then, and Gary brought a new level of chaos to a situation that was already tumultuous.

One time while I was watching TV, he brought a sleeping bag into the room and positioned it between me and the TV—in other words, directly in my line of vision. He then proceeded to masturbate. I was scared to death and didn't know what to do.

When I was in the bathroom, Gary used a mirror to look at me under the bathroom door. Whenever I opened the door, he rapidly jumped to his feet and pretended he just walking by. Soon after that, he drilled small holes on one side of the bathroom door and larger ones on the other side, creating a peephole through which he could watch. Sometimes when I was cooking dinner in the kitchen, he went into the bathroom, turned the light off, and kept the door open far enough so he could see me. I was too disgusted to look at him but knew full well what he was doing in there.

Before too long, his peeping moved beyond the bathroom. One morning I came home really drunk to find a hole in my bedroom wall about the size of a nickel. It provided a perfect view of my room from the room Gary and my mom shared, which was on the other side of the wall. I was exhausted and just wanted to go to sleep, so I shoved a bunch of paper in the hole and went to bed. Hours later I woke up to the sound of him using a coat hanger to push the paper out of the hole. I yelled at him to stop his sick behavior before I jumped out of bed and left the house.

Once when Lucy's tall boyfriend was at our house, he accidentally touched the ceiling as we were goofing around.

Imagine our surprise when a pile of pornographic magazines fell out of their hiding place. Humiliated, we quickly gathered them up, put them away, and never said a word about them.

I was so scared of Gary, but he bought my alcohol for me—and I didn't want that to stop. Without him buying it, I had to stand in front of a liquor store alone trying to find someone willing to buy alcohol for me as an underage drinker. Those attempts were often unsuccessful, so I came to count on Gary.

At that point, I didn't remember Gary trying anything physical with me, but I was so afraid he would that I finally mustered up the courage to tell my mom all the things that had been going on. Her response was classic: "I talked with Gary, and we agreed he's got a lot of problems, but we're concerned about your drinking." As she had so often, she put all the blame on me.

Bill and I started dating frequently after that, and it wasn't long before he moved in with us. Soon after that, he and I got married in Reno. The wedding cost us only $20 back then; I have a picture of us there with a sign in the background that read, *Sorry, no refunds.*

We were drinking Everclear, and I don't remember much other than getting married, playing a few slot machines, and waking up in the back of my brother's El Camino once we were back home. They had all just left me there.

It took us a little while to get out of my mom's house and rent a duplex with Bill's sister, Diane, who ironically also had red hair, long and wavy. I didn't like Diane much; I was a bit jealous of her relationship with Bill. Had Gary not been involved, I may not have married so young. I was only eighteen, right out of high school after graduating two months early with *A*s and *B*s. Before Bill and I were able to move, I was considering getting a gun because I was so afraid of Gary and didn't know what he might do.

I soon became pregnant. I was still actively drinking and smoking pot before our first daughter was born. I remember packing my bags for the hospital, checking off the list of all the things they tell you to bring. Not surprisingly, what mattered most to me was alcohol—and the first thing I put in my bag was a dozen or so airplane-size Jack Daniels bottles.

I quit smoking pot soon afterward, as my body seemed to reject it. Whenever I smoked pot, I'd get high, then sweat like crazy—the pot would be out of my system in no time, and I'd be straight again. It just was no longer worth it. But I did keep drinking.

I don't often think about it, but Bill was abusive (but not as severely as Walt had been). When I first got pregnant with Brooke, I knew he had gone to a concert. I noticed the only $10 I had in my purse was missing, so we got into a huge argument. We had a rocking chair that sat very low to the ground because it was broken off at the base. He slammed me into the chair. I had the wind knocked out of me, and it felt like my spine had just shrunk to about an inch from my neck to the middle of my back. I did end up going to a chiropractor, but they couldn't take x-rays or do any treatments because I was so far along in my pregnancy.

Another time Bill got really mad at me while we were in bed, and he hit me in the head. It was dark, and I was turned on my side. Luckily, I wasn't on my back, or he would have hit me in the face.

He tried to try to get me to engage in a threesome on several occasions, but it never happened.

He was a liar and a cheat. He had money taken out of his bank account and put into some kind of savings that I didn't know existed so he could buy drugs, which he was doing a lot of at this time. He once told me the more I complained about it, the more money he took out.

He also hid porn all over the house. If I found it and got mad, he'd just say, "That's why God made women so beautiful," or "What am I supposed to do, just poke my eyes out?" He always made me feel *I* was the one at fault.

Overall, Bill and I were happy until I discovered his cheating. I knew about three affairs that he willingly admitted to; I'm sure there were countless others. Once Bill told me he was spending the night at a guy friend's house—but when I called him, I could hear a little girl crying in the background. I knew that one of the girls he worked with had a little girl. When I confronted him, he admitted the affair, going into explicit detail about their night together. Then he asked me, "Can I still call her? Can I still go over to her house, and can I still be friends with her?"

I was baffled!

After hearing the details about his affair, I took him to work very early in the morning and stopped on the way home to buy some beer. Then I proceeded to get very drunk. I wrote him a letter telling him to get out; I waited at the neighbor's house next door to see what he would do.

He did move out. I was afraid he would come back in the middle of the night while my daughter and I were sleeping, so I slept on the floor by her crib. Sure enough, one morning I woke up to him with the telephone cord wrapped around his hands, saying he was going to tie me up. I finally convinced him I was going to comply but told him he was making me so nervous that I needed to smoke a cigarette first. On the way to get the cigarette, I escaped out of our living room window, which would never close all the way, and ran into our manager's house at 6:30 a.m. without even knocking. Thank goodness they were awake, and their door was unlocked.

The cops came, but Bill was already gone. He had punched several of the numbers out of the push-button phone and taken the coil wire and distributor cap off the Challenger so the car wouldn't run. He was planning a way to entrap me and make it impossible for me to escape by calling 911 or to get away in the car.

While pregnant, I was addicted to Ativan. I prayed every day that my daughter would be born healthy. Thank God she was, despite my use of drugs and alcohol. By then I wanted to stop drinking and using prescription drugs, but I no longer felt I had a choice. I had to use just to survive. I remember waking up one morning taking a drink of Black Velvet—it was cheaper than my preferred Jack Daniels— and chasing it with beer. I was shaking so badly. I felt sick, so I took deep breaths, trying to hold it in, only to throw up.

I repeated the same process over and over again just in an attempt to feel normal.

I once left Bill to live with a lady I knew because we were too broke to afford a doctor and medications, so I left him to qualify for welfare. Once on welfare, I got medical care and prescriptions for free. But I wanted to die, and I called him and told him so. Somehow, he found me, and I was so drunk and drugged that he tried to make me vomit; I bit his fingers. I left by ambulance and ended up in the hospital's mental ward. They had a seventy-two-hour hold on me for attempting suicide, but I told them what they wanted to hear and was released early. I even got my pills refilled by my doctor. It was so easy getting pills back then. At five months, I dressed as a fat person so I wouldn't look pregnant, and I got more pills then as well.

That was the first time a medical professional ever told me I was an alcoholic. When the doctor asked me how I was feeling, I simply shrugged my shoulders in reply. He said, "Pretty shaky, huh? You're an alcoholic." I brushed it off, as I had already proven to myself that I wasn't when I went those four days without drinking. At the time, I didn't know there are many kinds of alcoholics and that not all of them drink daily.

Bill anally raped me three to five times when I was passed out drunk. I didn't remember the rapes, but I found Vaseline in places it shouldn't be. When he knew I had caught him, he just told me it was my fault for getting so drunk.

After I kicked him out, Bill stayed out of the house we were living in. I ended up taking our daughter and moving into the same apartments where my mom lived. The complex was *U*-shaped with a pool, mail center, and laundry in the middle. So, there I was, a single, drunken mom.

At a time when I was so dependent on alcohol that I couldn't even go outside and check the mail without first taking a drink, Bill came over one day to grab some of his things. He was in a hurry, but I had just woken up from a blackout; I didn't know when I had last fed my poor daughter, but at least her diaper was dry. However, she had climbed up onto the center island between the living room and kitchen, and there was a broken glass on the countertop. That's when I knew I had had enough. I wanted to talk to Bill, but he wanted to get out of there as soon as possible. I kept begging him to talk to me, but he left the apartment, so I followed him.

My apartment was near the back of the complex, and I followed him as he hurried past the pool. I noticed everyone around the pool was staring at me just as Bill started to run. *I must look like a mess for just coming out of a stupor*, I thought, so I looked down to see what I was wearing. I was stark naked. I turned and ran back to the safety of my apartment.

I was so sick and tired of being sick and tired that I called Bill's uncle, who worked with the United Way; even though it was late at night, I asked him to take me somewhere right then. I spent the next thirty days in rehab. We had to do chores, cook, and clean. There were cockroaches all over the place. It was considered skid row—the drunks who had hit the lowest bottom ended up there, and that pretty much described me. In fact, I spent my twenty-first birthday in rehab. (Just a note: I have now been sober for thirty-six years. I never relapsed with my drinking—though I repeatedly relapsed with abusive men, eating disorders, smoking, and OCD.)

While I was in rehab, I desperately wanted to leave because I was convinced my poor baby daughter needed me. I did try to leave three times; however, each time another patient grabbed onto me, preventing me from leaving until I talked to a counselor. The counselors always persuaded me to stay by reminding me that I wouldn't be any good to my daughter unless I took care of myself first, so I stayed.

During the time I was in rehab, Bill moved into my apartment, saying he did so to take care of our daughter. Once I got home, it took me three weeks to clear my brain and even remember any of his affairs. I was also anorexic at the time, but I had an unexpected experience: after eating three meals a day for three weeks in rehab, I was embarrassed about how skinny I was. Earlier, I wouldn't even go out to check the mail without wearing long pants, even in the heat of the summer, because I thought my legs were so fat.

By the time I got out of rehab, we both wanted to go to college. We could afford tuition for only one of us—and Bill decided that since he was the smarter of the two of us, he should be the one to go. I knew I wanted another baby, and I wanted both of my children to have the same father—so even though I wasn't sure we'd stay together, I decided to become pregnant. Bill still drank a lot, but he was nice enough never to drink at home. He was just never home.

While I was pregnant, my brother and I drove from California to Texas to see our dad. I flew back home with my toddler in tow and five months pregnant with my second baby. That trip became a life-changer for me: while in Texas, I discovered that my mom had tried to kill me—not once, but twice.

Regarding the first incident, I grew up being told a story of the house we lived in. I was told that she was scrubbing the bathroom floor with gasoline, and it caught on fire. That was all I ever knew. On that trip to Texas, however, my dad told me he had come home from work unexpectedly only to find me strapped into my baby seat in the bathroom, the place in flames. My mother and my brother were simply standing outside the bathroom. My father saved me.

Once I realized she tried to kill me that day, things started making sense. Why would she use gasoline to scrub the bathroom floor? Even if she had, it wouldn't have been enough to start a fire. That's not all: there was never any evidence of her hands being burned, which they would have been had it happened as she said it did. And why would any mother have an infant with her where there were going to be heavy gasoline fumes?

The second incident happened when I was three. My mom said I drank my dad's lighter fluid and had to get my stomach pumped at the emergency room. Through later trauma therapy, though, I clearly remembered standing on the side of the tub holding my father's lighter fluid. I remembered too that my mother told me to get it out; she then pinned me down on the ground and squirted the lighter fluid in my mouth. I subsequently described the tin can to my husband, and he confirmed that I had perfectly described what lighter fluid cans looked like back then.

When I returned from my two-week trip to Texas, I came home to find that Bill had changed the sheets. At first, I thought nothing about it. I later learned that he shared our bed with a coworker. About that time, I found a little card on the floor of our car; I still remember the exact words: *You bring sunshine to my life; have a nice day.* It was signed by Rhonda, his best friend's wife. (Later, Bill was threatened with going to court for a paternity test regarding Rhonda's baby.)

After I had my second daughter, I thought the reason he was never around was that I hadn't lost all my fat from the pregnancy, so I went on an extremely strict diet, allowing myself only eight hundred calories a day. It took a bit longer to lose the birth weight the second time, especially since both my daughters were bottle-fed; there were times I was so hungry and I wanted to eat so badly that I cried. But I persevered—swapping one addiction for another—and I finally reached my goal.

To my surprise, though, nothing changed with Bill. I then thought maybe I hadn't lost *enough* weight, so more and more came off. Before long, I was anorexic again. My mother said I looked like a prisoner of war, but I thought I still looked fat. My mind was so twisted that I loved her "compliment"—it meant I was doing something right.

After a year or so of starving myself, I just couldn't do it anymore. Many times, I wanted to eat so badly that I cried for hours and hated the fact that I couldn't eat. At that point, the bulimia kicked in and became totally out of control for several years. Bill once told me I looked like death warmed over, a comment that made me sparkle from within, gloating with glee about my progress.

Bill had a pattern of moving out every summer so he could party and run around with other women. Divorce wasn't an option then because I missed him like crazy. I believe now I was missing him in advance knowing somewhere in my being we'd divorce.

When I asked Bill to move out for the last time, it was so strange. It was as if someone was speaking through me, and as I was asking him to leave, I kept thinking, *Shut up, dummy; he's going to really do it*. I kept fighting it, but the words just flowed.

I'd had enough, and I decided to divorce him.

After the divorce, while we were swapping kids for the weekend, I saw a picture of a naked woman on Bill's wall. Even though I was very drunk, I refused to leave the kids with him. He got extremely angry, and as I sped away, he threw his car keys at the back of my car, breaking the taillight. He then jumped into his vehicle, and the chase was on.

I was terrified: an enraged, drunken ex was chasing me down, and I didn't know what to do. I decided to drive into town and go to the police station. Once he figured out where I was going, he quickly disappeared.

I was finally able to quit smoking. Missionaries from The church of Jesus Christ of Latter-day Saints had tried everything to help me for the past five years, but I quit for good just three weeks after I got rid of Bill.

In all fairness, Bill did have some good qualities, and I did truly love him—but I feel I would have loved him much more had I not still had feelings for Walt. Bill and I were married for six and a half years, and it took six months to get a divorce in California back then. After the divorce was finalized, I called Walt. I finally got an apology from him for breaking my jaw. But after going out several times, I didn't know what I had ever seen in him to begin with. I was the one who then called the whole thing off—something I never thought I'd do after being so devastated over our first breakup. I finally learned I was no longer in love with him; instead, I was in love with the memory of what we had seven years earlier. I knew we'd never get it back, and I knew I was finally over him.

I've often had a sixth sense about things, and sometimes experienced things that seemed to be *déjà vu* or warnings. Right after I divorced Bill and quit smoking, I started walking the Sacramento River Trail. I was a speed walker; others walked, jogged, or skated. There was no bridge yet, so I could only go back and forth on either side, and I took a route that totaled about five miles.

One day while walking along listening to my Walkman, I noticed that the flowers, grass, water, and everything else around me were exceptionally vivid and vibrant in color. I was in awe. About halfway along my route, I saw in my mind's eye a woman in a garbage bag at the side of the trail. It shook me a bit, but I continued on my way.

The next time I was walking the trail, the same vision happened again at the same spot on the trail. A warning voice that seemed to say *Beware* caught my attention. I was a bit more shaken that time and continued walking, but I was looking over my shoulder and checking out spots where someone could hide.

The third day I was nervously walking on the trail when at the same spot I saw the same vision. This time, the voice seemed to be loudly saying, *GO BACK*. I turned and ran back to my car as fast as I could. I never walked the trail alone again; a guy friend from AA walked it with me. If he couldn't go, I just went around my neighborhood.

One day about three weeks after my warning experience on the trail, I was walking through the neighborhood listening to the radio when the announcer said they had just found the body of a woman near the Sacramento River Trail. I often wondered if that could have been me had I not heeded the warnings I was given.

CHAPTER SIX

There I was, a twenty-five-year-old divorced mother of two little girls. I had always been a stay-at-home mom, so I ended up going on welfare to survive, just as I had every time Bill and I split up.

Things were a mess. Bill never came around, but I never really expected him to. After all, my dad was never around after my parents split up, so why should Bill be there for me? Then one day the county got hold of him about paying child support. He told me, "Well, if I'm going to have to pay for them, I might as well see them." What a sad sentiment.

Now that I was sober, I hated men. Don't get me wrong: I didn't limit my hatred to Bill; I hated all of them. Someone in AA said that if you have resentment toward someone you should pray for that person—even if you don't want to—because it will make the resentment go away. I *really* didn't want to pray for Bill, and I had my doubts about the whole idea, but I was also sick of the hatred that was building up inside me. So, I tried it.

After two weeks, as promised, the hatred was gone. I prayed for good things for him. At first, I didn't mean a word of what I had said, but the anger gradually lessened until I was finally able to come to peace with the situation and forgive him.

Once that happened, we became close friends. We met to exchange the kids and had lunch together, hugging and exchanging "I love you" as we departed. It was no longer a romantic kind of love, and we were both remarried, but there was no hatred or resentment between us.

I learned through this experience that when I felt anger, I was hurting only myself, which was why I was willing to try prayer. I've found it to work every single time; I've been able to let go of resentment and anger toward others and give it all to God. He is much more capable of handling it than I am. He takes the burden from my shoulders, but only after I humble myself enough for Him to do so.

Letting go of my hatred toward men was a life-changing experience. After being clean and sober for four years, I slowly started dating several men in the program, but it never seemed to work out—probably because I was nowhere near ready to commit. The exception to that was a man named Paul. He and I became best friends, but that's all we could be. When I was separated from Bill, Paul would be back with his wife, and vice versa. A few times we were both single, and I thought my relationship with Paul might actually go somewhere.

I'd joined The Church of Jesus Christ of Latter-day Saints about that time. My values and morals changed, and so did my relationship with Paul, although we remained the closest of friends for a very long time. Three weeks after I got rid of Bill, I was finally able to stop smoking, as I mentioned.

And three weeks after I stopped smoking, I was baptized a member of the Church on October 17, 1987.

When I quit smoking, I still wasn't sure that I was going to divorce Bill. Divorce had never really crossed my mind, even though I grew up thinking my parents were divorced. As I contemplated what to do, I sought a priesthood blessing. On the way home, I heard "In Too Deep" by Phil Collins on the radio, and I knew what I had to do. Some of the lyrics really touched my soul; they reflected my feelings—I had given Bill too many reasons for his inappropriate behavior, believing he would always be there. But I was playing for keeps, and I could no longer take it.

I often get powerful inspiration when I hear a song on the radio that gives me the direction I need to go, and I knew this was one of those times.

Most people get irritable and short-tempered when they stop smoking, but that didn't happen to me. I was on such a spiritual high it was amazing. It was exhilarating. It was like the happiest moment of my life multiplied a hundredfold and nonstop for three full days. It was too much. I was too high to sleep; it was exhausting. After the third day, I had to pray for that feeling to go away; it was more than I could handle. God answered my prayers, and the intensity did go away.

Quitting smoking wasn't all roses and chocolate. It did get very hard at times, but thanks to the American Cancer Society and the pamphlets I'd picked up, I knew what to expect, so I was able to hold on through the roughest times, knowing it would get better. The actual urge to light up lasts only about fifteen to twenty minutes. Days three through five are usually the worst, with anxiety, depression, agitation, and many other symptoms. The brain fog for me was horrible. I couldn't even think and became very agitated.

Those symptoms did lessen over time. I knew I wanted to get married in the temple to the man I saw in my dreams three times while still married to Bill, long before I ever even imagined divorcing him. Because of that, I knew I had to be willing to do whatever it took to get to where I wanted to be.

As there were next to no guys from church around to date, I dated men from the program. The last thing I needed was a guy with a lot of baggage! I had a best friend everyone called "In-and-Out Kevin" because he couldn't stay sober and was always in and out of the program. To me, he was "safe," because they also recommend you don't get into a relationship for at least one year after getting sober, so I knew we would never be more than friends.

I never had so much fun in my life as I did with Kevin. He was tall, dark, and handsome. A woman from church once asked if he was my boyfriend when I brought him to a church activity. I said no. The woman said he was sure cute enough to be a boyfriend. Oh, how looks can be deceiving.

We did so much together. We went to a club where there was drinking, but we stayed sober; he talked me into dancing, which I greatly feared, but I had the time of my life. We went to the movies and laughed so hard. We went to the fair and rode the Zipper; when it got to the top and stopped, we were upside down, and he kissed me. I later asked him what that was all about. He said he just wanted to see what it was like to kiss someone upside down.

I was pretty sure he'd never make it to a year of sobriety, so when he asked if I would marry him when he reached that year, I said yes. I eventually moved from Redding to Ukiah, and I never found out whether Kevin made it to a year.

My mom picked out an apartment for me in Ukiah before I ever saw it, but it was what I could afford. It had been very nice but was now so overrun with drug dealers and perverts that I wouldn't let my little girls go out to play. One of the neighbors flashed the kids as they walked by; others puked their guts out in the parking lot. We had shootings and were once escorted back to our apartment with an order to stay there for twenty-four hours.

The swimming pool was full of sand. There were cockroaches everywhere—on our toothbrushes when we brushed our teeth and on the breakfast plate I once served my daughter. It was horrible. We never unpacked, and I began searching for a new place after less than a week. The low-income apartments in Ukiah had a two-year waiting list but I applied anyway.

I received a priesthood blessing from my home teacher, and in the blessing, I was promised that housing for me would open up within thirty days. After returning from a trip to Disneyland with my mom, I listened to my answering machine. Miraculously, they had an opening just twenty-eight days later.

Just before the new apartment opened up, I was so desperate to get out of my current situation that I took Jenny and Todd, friends from church, with me to Redding to get apartment applications. Jenny had short, brown-grayish hair and was much older than I was, but she announced once that she needed help cleaning her apartment to get it ready for a HUD inspection. I volunteered to help, and we soon became good friends.

I saw Todd across the room one Sunday. He was also tall, dark, and handsome, but his cowboy hat totally threw me off. He looked nicer when he wore a baseball cap, but he was prematurely balding, so he didn't look good without some kind of hat. I was so shallow that I looked from the outside in, instead of the other way around; otherwise, he was awesome! He was always there for me to do guy things like fix my treadmill or just hang out as a friend.

We had stopped all over Redding the day we went to find applications; it was 104 degrees outside, and my car had no air conditioning. To cope with the heat, we purchased snacks and drinks. When I cleaned out all the garbage from our day of binging, I accidentally threw out all the applications I had gotten. When I discovered my mistake, I was beyond devastated. I felt I would be trapped in Ukiah forever.

Most of the guys I dated didn't seem to be my type. I broke it off with the few who were once things started getting serious. I didn't realize at the time what I was doing. I was scared to get into another bad relationship, so I stayed out of them altogether while telling myself there was nothing I wanted more.

Todd and I had one real date. We went out for Chinese food, and it was so awkward and uncomfortable for us both that we decided we could only ever be best friends. I might have been the one who decided that—I had heard from another guy in our singles group that Todd liked me and was determined to get me. That never happened.

Instead, I ended up meeting Brad at a church dance, even though I was with Todd that night. Though Todd and I were only friends, Brad had no way of knowing that. Brad and I met at the refreshment table, and he had no problem at all conversing and playing the good little Mormon boy. I danced with Brad a few times, and we exchanged numbers. He had black hair and a medium build. Though he said he was six feet tall, that wasn't true; he was closer to five-foot-eight.

Brad lived in Santa Rosa, which was an hour and twenty minutes south of Ukiah. My friends and I from Ukiah often went to the dances in Santa Rosa, which is where I met Brad. After he got my number, he began calling right away. Cell phones weren't yet on the market, and one month we had a $300 phone bill.

At first, I felt a little safer with Brad for several reasons. First, he had custody of his five-year-old daughter, so I assumed he must be a good guy; courts don't usually award custody to troubled parents. Second, he used to be a cop, and back then most cops were good, at least in my eyes. Finally, and most importantly for me, he was a member of my church. There were very few to choose from in that part of northern California.

But the blush quickly faded.

I told him once I was having a birthday party for my daughter at the skating rink, and he invited himself and his daughter to the party. I didn't even want him there, but I was too much of a doormat to stand up for myself and speak my truth.

At a subsequent church dance, I asked a number of my friends to ask Brad to dance so I could dance with other guys. After all, I went to the dance to meet guys and have fun, not to be with Brad. Sadly, Brad kept pushing himself on me. He was so persistent!

Another time, I drove my daughters to Redding—and of course, he invited himself along, so I wasn't able to see all the friends I had been planning on seeing, including Paul. We ended up staying in separate bedrooms with another friend of mine from the church.

I felt like Brad was suffocating me. I told him so and asked him to back off—to give me some space. My plea fell on deaf ears. Since he refused to honor my request, I finally broke it off with him. I felt so good about my decision; being apart felt so right.

Then Brad came over once to "talk," and the rest is history—the beginning of my seventeen years in hell. I used to wonder why God never warned me about Brad, but He did; things felt so right while we were apart, which was my answer—but I allowed Brad to persuade me otherwise.

My friend from church, Jenny, had a friend named Jason in Santa Rosa, and the four of us went on double dates. Jenny and Jason eventually got married in the Oakland Temple but later divorced. While we were all dating, Jenny had us over for dinner one night, and Brad was bragging about being a cop. He showed us all a scar on his shoulder where he had once gotten shot.

Brad took me to meet his family and his ex-wife when he picked up his daughter; it was as if he wanted to rub me in her face. She had divorced him and remarried, and she and her new husband had a little boy. His ex-wife was very pretty, with short, light-brown hair and a beautiful smile; she was also very thin, and I envied that. Brad used to say that she weighed ninety-eight pounds soaking wet.

Soon after that, Brad asked me to marry him. I was in love with the idea of being in love and getting married, but I was not in love with him. We decided to get married in September, which was four months away, but that felt too soon for me. I still was nowhere ready to commit, even after five years of being single.

My stepfather had been killed in a construction accident, and my mother received a settlement as a result. My mom gave me and my brother, Jim, each $60,000 from her share of the settlement. I bought a used car and some nice furniture and things for my apartment. I had more than $50,000 left after those purchases.

Brad decided that since we agreed we'd live in Ukiah, he wanted his daughter to start going to school there right away. She started living with me and my two girls way before Brad and I even married. I resented that—it was all too soon, and I had enjoyed being single and living alone. I was in no hurry to remarry. Besides that, she was already calling me *mom*, which created a lot of pressure.

Brad physically pushed himself on me, and we went a little further each time until one day I told him I thought we ought to go see the bishop. I felt we had crossed over some critical boundaries. But Brad said we were fine. Since he was such a "good priesthood holder" and member of the church, I let it go.

Sadly, we had sex shortly after that.

Brad's response was, "Now we have to get married as soon as possible to make it right." At that point, I didn't think I had any other choice. We had a quiet marriage in the bishop's office. My mom, Brad's dad, and four of our friends were there. Our goal was to marry in the temple, but because we had premarital sex, we had to wait one year after being civilly married to go to the temple. (Once the year was up, we did exactly that.)

I had a good friend from the program named Janet. She was one of the first people I met in AA in Ukiah. She had a very pretty face but was full-figured; she seemed an odd match to her fiancé, who was lean and ran a lot. She was going to get married about the same time I did, and we shopped for wedding dresses together.

Janet was driving home from work in Hopland one day when she was hit head-on by a seventy-seven-year-old alcoholic who was trying to commit suicide. He lived; she died, leaving behind her three-year-old son. Her little boy ended up having to go back to Texas to live with his father, who was a drug addict. Janet had been clean and sober for four years.

Right after Brad and I got married in the bishop's office, we went straight to Janet's funeral, then to her celebration of life, then straight to our honeymoon in Fort Bragg, California, by the ocean. I was wearing a red dress—appropriate, so I thought, for a wedding, funeral, celebration of life, and honeymoon, all in rapid succession. That should have been an omen.

After our honeymoon, we had a wedding reception. It was beautiful; we had a gorgeous cake, and lots of delicious refreshments, including quiche and watermelon halves filled with fruit. I was surprised at how many nice gifts we received, most of which I still have.

At my reception, a friend asked me if I really loved Brad. I said yes—in truth, I was thinking, *No, but in time I'll learn to love him.* That never happened: only one month into our marriage, the abuse began.

CHAPTER SEVEN

The name-calling began after just one month.

Soon after that, things got physical. There was also brutal emotional abuse. As just one example of that, when I first became pregnant with my son, Brad told me he hoped I would lose the baby because I didn't deserve another child.

Early in our marriage, I discovered why Brad had custody of his daughter—and it wasn't because he was such a good guy. I found out Brad was somewhat abusive to his ex-wife as well and punched holes in the walls when he was angry. She said she was scared to death of him at the time, and she never wanted to face him in court. *That's* how he ended up with custody of their daughter.

By the time we married, my bank wouldn't allow me to put Brad on my account due to his bad credit. He had a friend in Sebastopol who worked at a bank, and his friend was able to get us both on an account at a local bank in Ukiah. We used about $17,000 of the settlement money I had received from my mom as a down payment on our first house. I kept getting past-due notices from credit companies saying how much he owed. I had always had really good credit, and I hated being in debt, so I used my settlement money to pay them off. Brad always promised me there weren't any more, but they just kept coming, and I just kept paying.

While he was abusive, he wasn't what I would call a "serious abuser" in those early days; in other words, his abuse wouldn't put someone in the hospital, which is probably why I had a hard time seeing it for what it was. But abuse is abuse. One time he moved his arm a certain way and I flinched, thinking, *He is going to hit me.* The thought then occurred to me that he was going to become physically abusive. I was right.

There was verbal abuse early in our marriage as well, including lying. We went with groups of friends to the Oakland Temple, and he bragged about all the things he did while he was in the Marines. He became extremely angry if I shut the door when I went to the bathroom, saying things like, "When I was in the Marines, we'd just dig a hole and go to the bathroom wherever we were, and it didn't matter who was around." (I knew never to lock the door because I learned more than once he'd break it down.) It was only later that I found out from his mother and sister that he was never in the Marines.

I soon realized was a pathological liar. The lies were pervasive, about anything and everything. Brad claimed he was fired from the police force because he punched the police chief. And remember the scar on his shoulder he said he sustained from a gunshot wound while on the police force? Brad's ex-wife told me he was never even a cop. The scar on his shoulder wasn't from a gunshot wound; it happened when he and his best friend were out drinking and driving, and his friend crashed the car, leaving Brad in a coma and paralyzed from the waist down for a month. Doctors told him at that time he'd never walk again.

My mom warned me that if he lied to me as our marriage began, he'd always tell me lies—maybe not big ones, but he'd always be a liar.

She was right.

Brad was also a control freak. When it came to me and the kids, he had to control everything everyone did—from what we ate to how much ketchup we used and even how much fun we were allowed to have. He often went into uncontrollable rages. I remember once while I was nursing my oldest son, Brad started screaming and yelling until his eyes bulged out and the sweat was running down his face. My son somehow fell asleep in the middle of it all. I believe now that his little spirit went back to heaven so he could get away from it for a while.

Brad's abuse played out in so many ways. We were in our master bathroom once and he started punching the wall all around my head, putting five large holes in the wall; it scared me to death. A highway patrolman lived nearby; I knew him and his family from church, and I went to stay with them, explaining that I didn't know what I was going to do. Somehow, Brad discovered where I was staying. He called and asked to talk to me, and we ended up back together. It was my first attempt at leaving him. I did pursue a restraining order but ended up getting back with Brad before it went through.

He choked me during the first year whenever I mentioned the word *divorce*. I hated him by then so badly. I almost passed out each time he choked me, and I truly believed each time I was going to die. Finally, when I saw him coming at me, I told him I loved him, hoping it would keep him from choking me. I wanted a divorce throughout our entire marriage, but after that first year, I learned not to express those thoughts.

I was not in a good situation to make it on my own. I was too afraid to work because my mother had instilled in me the belief that I was not good enough in any way; I just knew that I would miserably fail at whatever I attempted. I couldn't get on welfare, as I had when Bill left me, because I still had about $10,000 of the settlement money.

Just before I got pregnant with my first son, I had a miscarriage. Brad was out of town on work-related business and didn't seem too upset by the whole ordeal, yet I could tell he was a bit disappointed—probably because having a child with him would be a way for him to hold on to me.

The abuse got worse, as it always does. I had to train my two older daughters how to call 911 in case Brad ever got really bad and out of hand and I needed help. During the early years of our marriage, I didn't have a cell phone, so my daughters and I had to make all our calls on the house phone. During my second pregnancy, he was horrible, even worse than he had been the first year. He once hit me in the head, knocking me on the ground. The neighbors who saw the incident called the police, but I again protected my abuser because I was afraid I couldn't make it on my own.

As I nursed the baby, Brad slapped me across the face and thought nothing of it. I did call the police once, but nothing was ever done. He also threw the remote control at my face when I was very pregnant with our second son and split my eyebrow open. He then took me to the emergency room—we made up a story about how I got lightheaded and hit my head against the corner of the wall as I passed out. Everyone there was joking with him about abusing his pregnant wife. I wonder now how many of those people had the slightest inkling that what they were joking about could have possibly been true.

Brad was like a time bomb, and I never knew what would set him off. Sometimes he exploded over obvious things, but other times it would be for no good reason at all. Our refrigerator had several dents in it from him punching it. Twice I saw him put his entire head through the bedroom wall. Sometimes he punched himself in the head over and over again until he had big lumps on his head.

He once hit my oldest daughter in the mouth, and I ran over to our neighbor friends and called the police. The highway patrolman I had stayed with was one of the officers who showed up; nothing was done, even though Brad left a mark. My daughter stayed with a friend that night, and Brad said the cops were even joking about smacking a mouthy teen; I don't believe that's what happened, but in Brad's mind, he did nothing wrong.

I once told a woman from church that I wanted a divorce. She had three adopted children—a girl, who was best friends with my oldest daughter, and two boys. The boys had a bad background and needed lots of help. She had gone through a therapy program with her boys that she thought would help us. Called "Holdings," the therapy involved wrapping us tightly in blankets, making it impossible for us to move, and then having us talk. During that therapy, I learned that what Bill had done to me was wrong: all the times I had been passed out, Bill had raped me. Even though I had been too drunk to resist, I had felt shameful and had taken the blame for it all. I also didn't consider my first few encounters with men as rape; it had always been that way when I was a little girl, so I considered it normal.

We stayed at the home of another church member for about three days while we started therapy, but we were just not comfortable there, so the bishop paid for us to stay in a motel. Our oldest son was just a toddler then. We pretended the therapy helped for a while, but soon everything was as bad as it had been.

We then tried some other counseling. We lived in Ukiah, and the counselor was in Santa Rosa; on the way, Brad drove like a jerk and swerved all over the road, speeding up and slamming on the brakes to scare me. One issue we discussed with the therapist was Brad getting mad when I wanted to bake an apple pie at ten p.m. The counselor asked, "So what?" Brad then insisted that was the time I belonged in bed and I should be there with him instead of baking a pie. I learned during that session that *should* is a control word.

I finally slipped the counselor a note and asked if we could talk alone; it's difficult to discuss issues with your abuser sitting right there. When we spoke privately, the counselor told me that if it were him, he wouldn't stay. He'd get out. He said that what we had didn't qualify as a marriage; it was a dictatorship. Yet even then I stayed. Years later Brad told me he went to all the counseling only so I'd stay with him; he didn't believe in any of it.

I so clearly remember standing over the sink peeling peaches from our tree to preserve in bottles. Suddenly Brad exploded because I was taking too much of the meat from the peach and wasting it. Whenever I thought things were going okay, something blew up, and the devil himself came out of the blue.

Brad snored like crazy, and I couldn't sleep at all. I tried a few times to go sleep on the couch, and he'd yell at me to get back in bed. I was terrified. A few times I tried to gently nudge him and tell him he was snoring so loudly it was keeping me awake. He simply responded, "You're crazy—I'm not even asleep! I'm just lying here with my eyes wide open staring at the ceiling." Who was I to argue with him?

Brad's pathological lying didn't stop. While I was pregnant with our first son, Brad was out of work for a short time. He was a roofer and did really well in the spring and summer, but in the winter, we lived off credit cards because he wasn't able to work. During that pregnancy, we decided to file for government assistance, and I was alone filling out the papers. One of the questions asked if either of us had ever been in the military. I answered yes, of course. They required some kind of documentation, so I went home and asked Brad about it. He exploded, saying, "You weren't supposed to tell anyone! My mom and sister don't even know where I was.

It was top-secret government stuff." Of course, I believed every word at the time. He finally told me to just say I'd made a mistake and that he hadn't been in the military—yet privately he still insisted he had.

When we bought our house, he lied and told the mortgage company he made more money than he really did so we could qualify for the loan. Within three years, we were broke. I used my last $3,000 for Brad to go into business for himself. Still living off credit cards in the winter, we finally saw no other way out than to file for bankruptcy, which we did.

Once that happened, Brad decided that moving to Utah was a good idea, especially since he was such a "staunch Mormon." So off he went. I was loving life being apart from him. I got a phone call from him maybe once every other week, sometimes once a week, but nothing more.

However, I was also left to keep the house spotless while trying to sell it. I had five kids at home; three were older, but two were much younger. I managed to make it work. I was such a perfectionist that one of my friends called me *Mrs. Perfect House*. That's how it looked on the outside, anyway; I didn't realize it at the time, but I had to prove I was good enough. I also believe it was my way of letting others think that everything was perfectly fine.

Our house didn't sell after three months on the market, and Brad was desperate to get our little family back together. We leased a home in Utah with an option to buy. Brad came home, and half the ward was there to see us off and help us pack. We stayed in a hotel that first night.

Once on the road, the U-Haul truck that was towing Brad's little truck was going only twenty miles per hour on a seventy-mile-per-hour highway. It was pretty scary. We stopped at one of the first rest stops we saw and waited for five hours with five kids for the AAA guy to come—only to find that he brought the wrong battery. We finally got the U-Haul fixed, but it was the first time I had to feed the kids Honeycomb cereal out of the box for dinner.

It was a long drive, but it wasn't too bad for me and the girls; we drove behind Brad in our Astro van. He was much nicer to the boys then, so they rode with him. Patrick was only nine months old, and Zach was almost four.

I had seen the house we were moving into only via a video camera that Brad had. It was definitely a fixer-upper, but I really liked all the additional room. It was four levels, compared to the one level we'd had in California, and it had five bedrooms and a food storage room. I hoped that Brad would be less violent in our new home.

Sadly, that wasn't the case. He was just as mean and abusive in Utah as he had been in California. I realized that Brad was a pretty lousy husband, and I was scared to death of him; I lived every single day of my life in fear. When I was nursing a baby, he yelled and screamed and cussed me out or even slapped me across the face as if it were nothing. While I was pregnant with one son and holding another, he liked to kick me in the shins. He choked me more than a dozen times until I almost passed out; he also threatened to kill me. He forced me to look into his eyes when he spoke to me. He forced the girls to eat foods they absolutely hated, saying that he had to eat those things when he was younger. It was about this time I learned he had been abused by his father and beaten with buggy whips, extension cords, two-by-fours, or whatever else his father could find. (Incidentally, his sister told me she got beaten too, but she didn't turn out like Brad.)

Every holiday we arrived at his grandma's house along with his dad and mom, who were divorced; his stepfather; his sister and her husband; and anyone else who might show up. Once Brad's ex-wife showed up, but all of us got along except Brad. He didn't like her being there. Brad couldn't even talk to her on the phone without exploding into a major rage. (I was the one who always had to speak to her on the phone and drive their daughter to the infrequent visitations.)

Every holiday I'd stand in the bathroom telling myself, "This is it!" I vowed it would be the last holiday—whether Christmas, Thanksgiving, or whatever—that I would spend with Brad's family. Brad's dad smoked a lot and had a raspy, annoying voice; he once called the house in California, and I thought he was a prank phone caller. He later died from lung cancer. His mother—Brad's grandma—also smoked a lot and was on an oxygen machine. We all stunk like cigarettes by the time we got home.

Brad didn't seem to care who saw or heard him abusing me. During our first year of marriage, Brad couldn't even control his anger during a company Christmas trip. We were on a bus, and while we were sitting there, something triggered Brad. He loudly told me he wanted to bash my face through the window.

When we arrived in Utah, it seemed the whole ward was at our house to help us unpack.

Not long after we arrived, the bishopric wanted to meet us. Our boxes were still full, and we hadn't unpacked anything, but Brad quickly went around the living room going through boxes and pulling out pictures of family and Christ, placing them where they'd be seen. He was a show horse. Everything was for looks. Before the kids and I arrived, Brad worked in the Salt Lake Temple, so everyone assumed he was a great guy.

While we lived in California, we fought all the way to church and back. In Utah, the church was close by, so we didn't have that horrible tension. But Brad argued with me as we were walking down the hallway in the church—and as soon as we walked into the foyer, he kissed me and acted as if nothing ever happened. I despised him so much I hated kissing him. I could feel my spirit pulling away from him as my body got closer; it would struggle and fight to go the other way. I didn't want to be near him. I didn't want him touching me. The way he always pretended like nothing ever happened reminded me years later of a water and fire restoration company that advertised when they were finished, "It's like nothing ever happened." That's how Brad was all through our marriage.

During the five years we lived in Utah, I so wanted the husband I dreamed about so long before. While I was married to Bill, and long before I had any intention of divorcing him, I dreamed of my "future husband." In the three dreams I had about him, I wasn't allowed to see his face; I only knew how he made me feel. It seemed so real and was like a heavenly love—one stronger than anyone is capable of feeling on this earth. I believed God was going to give me this man. Part of me had believed that man was Brad—and that one day he'd change and become the man from my dream. The longer the abuse continued, however, I knew that the man from my dream wasn't Brad. I believed that one day when the timing was right, I would meet this awesome person, and I would know who he was by how he made me feel.

I clearly remember having a one-sided argument with God, even cursing at Him, telling Him how He had promised me something beyond my wildest dreams only to give me my worst nightmare. Little did I know as I sat in the boys' bedroom window looking out, watching the planes fly overhead, that the special someone I would one day meet was only about minutes away. It was the dream about him that kept me going. (I should note that he's everything I could ever have wanted, and I am so grateful for the little miracles I receive. He's lived in the house we are in for twenty-nine years; I joined him almost eleven years ago.)

Brad was only physically abusive during the first six or seven years of our marriage; then he was arrested. But he still had me totally under his control because of the fear he instilled in me. He no longer needed to use physical violence when mental, verbal, emotional, and spiritual abuse was at his fingertips.

One time we were all getting ready for church. He picked me up and carried me down the hallway. I got away from him, ran into the bathroom, and locked the door. My daughter called 911, as I had taught her to do. He broke the door down and pushed me up against the wall, bruising my back on the towel rack. Then he started choking me. Somehow, things stopped, and he suddenly said, "It's time to go to church." He acted as if nothing ever happened. So off we went, leaving the children behind because they didn't want to go.

We were late, so we sat in the hallway outside the bishop's office until they were finished passing the sacrament. Suddenly, the cops arrived. Shortly after that, the chapel doors opened, and the people on the end row could see us talking to the police, so we went outside. The police said it didn't matter if I pressed charges; they arrested Brad because they could see the choke marks on my neck. He was gone for only a couple of hours before he came home.

After that, he wasn't physically abusive, but he was very verbally and emotionally and mentally abusive to everyone—even his own daughter. He screamed and yelled and cussed at her, telling her how stupid she was because she was getting bad grades in math. He also fought with my girls until my oldest had her baby and moved to California to live with her dad. The neighbor must have heard Brad screaming at everyone because he brought over a pamphlet about being a good parent.

I spoke to my bishop after Brad was arrested. The bishop told me he had considered giving Brad a calling in the ward but had the feeling something evil just left his office when Brad left. This bishop and the ward pretty much helped me plan my second escape. I flew in my friend Todd, who was with me the night I met Brad, and he drove the U-Haul from

Utah back to California; I followed in the car with the kids. He had been one of my best friends, and even though we dated once, we never kissed. I have often wondered if that would have made any difference. I was so into how someone looked that I never focused on his inner qualities, which were awesome.

On the move back to California, I took Brad's daughter to her mother's house. At one time, she had told me she didn't want any more kids, as she had another child with her current husband. I was pleasantly surprised when she agreed to take her daughter back, and even seemed excited at the offer. I believe she was happy to have her daughter back.

When I arrived in California, I filed for another restraining order. I was embarrassed—the same girl who had helped me before helped me again. I pretty much waited for God to make everything happen. Little did I know I had to do my part.

Todd later told me that the reason I went back to Brad *again* was that God knew we had unfinished business.

We did.

CHAPTER EIGHT

Before I left Utah, I found Brad's daughter doing some unusual things, so I called her mom. I suspected sexual abuse of some kind. I knew she'd go in the hot tub naked with her grandpa all the time. I also knew that when I met him, Brad had a bunk bed—a small one on top and a larger one on the bottom. They both slept in the bottom bed. She was five years old then.

After I talked to Brad's ex-wife, I got a phone call from his sister. She told me Brad, who was two years older, had sex with her almost every single day from the time she was ten until she was about thirteen. She said he used knives and threatened her if she ever told. Of course, Brad denied all this once it came out in the open; he told his family she was crazy and she was already going to a psychiatrist—in reality, she and her husband were getting counseling.

Years later, Brad's sister told me she remembered it wrong—that it wasn't Brad who had sex with her repeatedly, it was one of his friends. A therapist later told me that she *might* have made that mistake if she had been three years old when the sexual abuse occurred—but no way would she make such a mistake at age ten. The therapist said she was either covering for him for some reason or he threatened her.

Before long, I went back to Utah—and back to Brad. The first thing we did was start fighting. It was Brad's way of trying to gain control. Shortly after that, I became pregnant. I always knew Brad and I would have a boy and a girl. I was so sure that when I was pregnant the second time and the ultrasound showed the baby was a boy, I told everyone it must have been some kind of mistake because I *knew* I was having a daughter. I had no doubt. I even talked about her to my mom and wrote about her in my journals.

As it turned out, that little girl was born six years later. I knew she was in heaven waiting to come down. Had she come to us before our little boys were born, though, we would have stopped having children. Luckily, we did have those little boys.

Brad's snoring was driving me crazy, so I tried sleeping on the couch only to have him come storming down the stairs demanding I get my butt in bed. Not long after that, I started sleeping on the floor by Patrick's side. Brad was fine with that. Patrick's room was on the same level as ours, and as long as I was on the floor like a dog and wasn't too comfortable, Brad was okay with it. I went through my entire pregnancy and the next pregnancy—seven years total—sleeping on the floor until Brad finally got his snoring fixed.

My awful husband soon became a horrible father as well. He slapped my oldest son on the face once at a church Christmas program and left a mark on his face. When one of my daughters stopped going to school, he somehow got her admitted to the psychiatric unit of Primary Children's Hospital.

After living in West Valley City, Utah, for five years, Brad lost his job with a major roofing company. Brad searched for a job a little, but most days he didn't seem to be trying. Maybe he was depressed. He finally got an offer, and the company flew him to Eufaula, Alabama, for an interview. We found a few nice houses we might like and spoke to the woman in one; she said she was the only white person in the entire area. We looked at the school our kids would be attending, and there were no other white kids in the school. But I trusted in the Lord that things would work out okay and we'd end up where we were supposed to be. The people seemed very friendly, and not long after that we received a welcome packet, fully expecting to move to Eufaula. We were just waiting to hear back following Brad's interview.

While we were waiting, Brad was suddenly offered an even better job in Broken Arrow, Oklahoma. We lived in Oklahoma on September 11, 2001. That day Zach was in school. I was at Albertson's with Patrick, my daughter Dani, my son Cameron, and a little girl I babysat. We were standing in the checkout line when I overheard the clerk talking to another customer about a bomb that had detonated at the World Trade Center. I asked what had happened, paid for my groceries, and it seemed we were glued to the TV set the next couple of weeks.

The next day, September 12, marked my anniversary of being clean and sober. But I couldn't be happy about it and didn't feel like celebrating when the whole world was watching this tragedy unfold.

Someone posted a sign in front of the elementary school that read, *Bless America*. The world was no longer saying *Merry Christmas* or honoring other holidays to respect those who didn't believe in God, but after several days I was so happy to see that they added the word *God* to the sign, which then said *God Bless America*. If we leave out God in our greatest times of need, we are really in trouble.

We had a nice house that was owned by the person who hired Brad. We were initially renting the house, but he was having a lot of money problems, so he tried to get us to buy the home. Thinking it would make his job more secure, Brad decided to buy it. Brad also made me sign the papers so that I'd be part owner of the house, even though I kept telling him I didn't want to. I was too scared to disobey him, though, for fear of what he might do if I didn't comply. One month later, his boss fired Brad with no concern for me or the children.

But we mostly loved our time in Oklahoma. We had a three-foot-deep above-ground pool put in, and the kids all loved it. Cameron was so not afraid of the water that it was scary. He'd just jump right in anytime. I made sure to keep the patio doors locked at all times, and he wore his arm floaters whenever he went outside to swim. Patrick once rode this big dolphin we bought, and I have a wonderful memory picture of him on it waving as if he were meant to be with the Dolphins from the beginning. When he died at the age of seventeen, he was doing the Dolphin Challenge in Galveston, Texas.

During three months of sheer terror, Brad was so mean and abusive to me that I wished I could die. I went into a major depression, without realizing at the time that it was so I'd know that if it was ever *really* bad that I did have a way out. I felt utterly hopeless and trapped. Every day I fantasized about putting my four youngest children in the car, going into the garage, and letting the car idle until we all just peacefully fell asleep, forever. My second daughter from my first marriage was older, so I imagined she'd be fine. My oldest had moved to California to get away from her boyfriend's family, who were trying to make her sign over the baby to them once she was born.

(Her boyfriend eventually moved in with her in California, getting her pregnant again; then they were married and had their third child. I am so proud of her for going to a special school for mothers and getting her diploma, even though she was two years behind.)

Brad hit my second-oldest daughter once while we lived in Oklahoma. He hit her in the face and left a bruise that she covered with makeup. Her boss at the daycare center where she worked recognized what had happened, and my daughter somehow managed to get her boss to keep quiet about the whole thing. My daughter was so worried about what might happen to me and the kids if Brad got put away.

The first night in the Oklahoma house we all slept in what they called the sunroom on the new carpet. The room, which they had built onto the house, had sliding glass doors for the walls and two large skylights. It wasn't until we were settled in for a bit and it began to rain that we found big, fat, long earthworms that had tried crawling across the carpet, had died, and had become shriveled and hard overnight. The plush new carpet was no longer inviting as a place to sleep!

It was here we began to suspect my youngest son, Cameron, had autism. He didn't talk until he was four. We started seeing bizarre behaviors. He once went on a three-week cottage cheese binge and refused to eat anything else; since then, he's never eaten cottage cheese. When he had cheese puffs, he'd eat the end of each one, one at a time. Then he'd eat the other end, one at a time. Then he'd eat the middle parts. But he *always* left one whole cheese puff on his plate. The odd behaviors weren't limited to food. He put things at the top of the stairs and curiously watched them fall. He made what we called "crop circles" on the floor with his diapers.

Cameron is the only one of our kids who went to pre-K, and we put him through kindergarten twice. One day while teaching some of the other kindergarteners their ABCs, the teacher caught Cameron doing some independent reading. He had taught himself to read from the times we had held him on our laps and read books to him.

Cameron was also a C-section baby, and I can't help but wonder if the complications during his birth are somehow related to his autism. After Dani's birth, I was told I would be tempting fate to have another baby. I cried all the way home, even though we didn't particularly expect to have more children. We prayed about it, and I knew I had one more coming—and that it would be the last one.

A normal C-section takes about half an hour from start to finish. Mine took an hour and a half, even though it was done by a prominent perinatal specialist who focused on high-risk pregnancies and emergency C-sections. I had been going to a midwife throughout my pregnancy, but midwives don't do C-sections, so when it became obvious that I needed one, that doctor got called in. Had I had any other doctor, I probably would have died.

They had given me spinal anesthesia instead of an epidural, and it started to wear off during the surgery. When I said, "Ouch!" the doctor said, "You can't be feeling that." But I was. The anesthesiologist wasn't sure what to do, so they put Ketamine in my IV.

That's when the hallucinations began.

At first, everyone's faces looked Asian. Then everyone in the room had on big party hats. Then I saw life full of kaleidoscopes. I started repeatedly asking the doctor, "I'm dead, aren't I? Am I dead?"

Later he pulled me aside and said, "I didn't want to say this in front of your husband, but yours was one of the most difficult C-sections I have ever done."

Cameron is now twenty. He graduated high school and is still living at home. He's still a strange kid, but we love him to pieces—and, just as many of his teachers told us over the years, he is brilliant.

Zach turned eight in February. Not enough people showed up that we could have him baptized, so we had to make some phone calls to get the witnesses we needed. After living in Utah for five years, where baptisms were always very well attended, I thought this was pretty ridiculous. We finally got him baptized. I knew Brad wasn't worthy to perform the baptism, but I also knew the Lord wouldn't hold it against Cameron and that it would still be valid in His eyes. One day Brad will be held accountable for all of the things he's done.

Brad offered to help my brother out at one point by getting him a job where he worked. My dad had died, so my brother and his eleven-year-old son left Texas and moved in with us. I took him only because of the pleadings of my mother. She was still always helping her "golden child."

Things rapidly went downhill. My brother drank every day, but we made him keep his alcohol in the garage. We also found a lot of porn on the computer after he used it. My brother was lazy and didn't do the work well when they did find something for him. After he had lived with us for six weeks, I was at my wits' end. I was surprised one day when walking out to my car alone the fleeting thought crossed my mind that I could steal one of his beers and no one would ever know. I had gone to only one AA meeting during our year in Oklahoma, and I was now reminded how cunning, baffling, and powerful alcohol can be.

On Halloween, my brother threatened to beat his son, knocking over Cameron in the process and shouting a tirade of crude words. That was the last straw—I decided he had to go. He had been fired from his job, so he applied for welfare, and we helped him move to Tulsa. I spent a lot of money buying them plenty of groceries so they wouldn't starve. I still feel bad for him and all the poor choices he's made in his life that led him to where he is. It's so sad watching alcohol consume a person. (I am so humbled and grateful to have recently celebrated thirty-seven years of sobriety. Even though I broke all the rules and made some terrible decisions of my own, I still haven't taken that first drink.)

As the time approached for Brad to go back to Texas, he went ahead to look for a house while we stayed in Oklahoma to sell the house in which we had been living. We ended up doing another lease with an option to buy, hoping to get rid of that house and get away. As Brad got ready to leave, I closed my eyes and wrapped my arms tightly around my body as if to somehow comfort myself. My arms felt like a barrier protecting me, at least momentarily. I could feel my throat tighten, yet I didn't dare let out a sound for fear of what might happen if Brad heard me and knew of the fear that enveloped my entire being.

The smell of fresh-baked bread coming from the bread machine gave me a sort of silent peace as if to say, "It's going to be all right." I bit my bottom lip and took in a deep breath, but I could no longer contain the emotions that had welled up inside me. Suddenly I burst into tears, and every emotion imaginable flooded my body.

"What is your problem?" Brad shouted. I had to think fast. I couldn't let him know that I was crying because I hated him so much for all the things he had done to me and my children over the years. He was an evil monster, and I felt validated in praying that he would die every time he boarded an airplane to go out of town. I felt so happy each day when he left, but the moment I heard his truck in the driveway I once again sunk into a fog of depression and despair.

I could taste the bile rising from my throat as I spurted out the only thing that came to mind: "I'm just going to miss you is all," I said. "I hate it when you're gone and I have to take care of the kids all by myself, and"—I almost choked over my final words—"I love you." I was sure he would pick up on my massive lie, but the idiot actually bought it. How could he even think for a second that it was true? But that's what he wanted to hear and what he needed to hear to know he had me in his control.

A sly smile crossed Brad's lips as he said, "I'll be back in two weeks."

I knew how horrible life would be again. I'd pick him up from the Tulsa airport, and during the twenty-minute drive to Broken Arrow, he'd make sure the kids and I knew he was back and that he was in control again and that we'd better listen to him and do as he said, or else. As soon as he'd get in the car, he would be fighting with one of the kids within just a few minutes, and by the time we reached home, he'd be raging. No one dared argue back.

We lived in constant fear, even though his physical abuse had become verbal, mental, and emotional (which can often be even worse). Brad no longer needed to hurt me with his hands or fist, as he could just as easily control me with his words.

I remembered a time not long before this where I was hopeless and so desperate to get away from him but knowing that was impossible. I'd tried it before and failed. Why did I keep going back to him, a man I never even loved to begin with?

Brad had strong-armed me into marrying him with his persistence. I didn't love him then, but I believed I would eventually grow to love him . . . someday. After all, he was a rare find. He was a member of our church, he had been a policeman, and he had custody of his daughter. He had to be a good guy even though the chemistry just wasn't there; it would surely come, eventually.

I had been in a deep depression for three months and couldn't shake it. I realized much later that this had been my coping mechanism so that I could deal with what was going on. I knew I could leave if I had to if and when things got bad enough. Of course, I would take the children with me. No way would I leave them behind with Brad. He was a sociopath and capable of anything.

One day I felt inspired to tell Brad how I was feeling; it was almost as if God Himself were speaking to me. The same thing crossed my mind three times, but I kept questioning it. I didn't understand how or why a loving God would want me to confess this to my abusive husband. However, I finally did as I felt prompted to do.

Brad simply turned to me and said, "You're just a miserable person; why don't you just go and kill yourself?" I could hardly believe the coldness of his comment. Looking back, I can only think God had me confess this to him so that someday he will be held accountable.

It seemed from day one I was always happy with everything in my life except who I was married to. I longed for that husband I dreamed about so long ago, and by now I realized Brad wasn't—and never could be—that person.

Brad terrified me, and I walked on eggshells in fear for my life every single day. I'd turn on the news and hear, "Mother of three killed; suspect is her husband." I'd imagine what picture they would use when it was my turn. I truly believed he was capable of killing me, and many times I thought he was going to as he had threatened to so many times the first year of our marriage.

Every time I mentioned divorce, he would start choking me until I almost passed out, so I learned to stop saying that word. However, I never stopped wanting one. I also never thought I'd actually be able to free myself of Brad by getting a divorce—though I finally did.

All in all, I'd do it over again, if nothing else than to have our wonderful children—especially Patrick, who died of lymphoma in 2013. I learned much from my seventeen years in an abusive marriage, and I hope that by sharing with others some of what I have learned I can help even one person to better understand why women go back. It's a normal reaction to an abnormal situation, and women who are trapped in it are not crazy. There is a reason for everything; I knew there was a purpose for all I had gone through and that one day I would see God's hand in all things. I had faith that I would understand to some degree why it all happened the way it did.

I had all the comforts of a nice home rather than trying to make it in a shelter or, worse, out on the street. I had everything I needed and just about everything I could ever want materially, so why leave all that not knowing if I could survive on my own and provide for my children? I was terrified to leave and terrified to come back, but at least I knew coming back meant some source of stability even if it put me in danger.

When Brad messed with me, I could take it; I was used to it. But once he started on the kids, I would leave—I always put my kids first—but I never seemed to be able to stay away. I disassociated and thought only of the good things about being back together and forgot all the bad. Once back, I immediately found myself wondering how I could have ever come back to all of this . . . AGAIN! Then I'd immediately start planning my next escape.

CHAPTER NINE

The day finally arrived: Houston, here we come! I was so excited! With Brooke in California with her dad and Aubrey in California with her mom, that left Jessica, Zach, Patrick, Dani, and Cameron.

The house we put $500 down on to be built wasn't ready yet, so we spent three weeks in a hotel. There wasn't much to do, and the kids became quite restless—but there was a pool, which helped. It was summer, and it was HOT! All of our belongings waited in the U-Haul for the day we could unpack.

We found another house we liked; we called it "The Plain Jane House" as we compared it to the elaborate one with the spiral staircase and all the upgrades in Atascasita—but it was finished and ready to move into. We wanted the fancy house, but looking back, the Plain Jane house was the best choice. It was a huge, three-story, four-bedroom, two-and-a-half-bath, gorgeous home in a lovely, verdant, wooded area with trails all along the cul-de-sacs that made up our subdivision. There was also a pool in the middle of the development.

As we were driving back and forth one day trying to decide on which house to get, we passed Ollie's Quickie

Picky. I had dreamed of this two-lane, drive-through store with its bright neon lights six months before I ever saw it. I had no idea such a thing even existed. I remember telling Brad about my dream and how in my dream, we had driven through to buy milk. As we passed that day, I yelled, "That's it—the store I dreamed about!" And I made him drive through.

We did go there on occasion but never to buy milk. I spoke to the guy running it and told him about my dream. He told us that to the best of his knowledge, it was one of a kind, and there was no other store out there like it. It contained last-minute items one might need like gas, milk, beer, and cigarettes. I drove past this store every time I went anywhere, as our house was at the end of that road.

As we were closing the deal on the house, Brad said the F-word to the realtor, right in front of me. He had no control over anything he did or the outrageous ways he reacted to even the slightest provocation. He wasn't a good example of the church or even of a human being due to how he reacted to things. However, things did get worked out, and we were able to move in.

The first day we were in our new home, the kids ran around like crazy having so much fun; I loved hearing all their laughter. I knew we were home. That's not all: they were tired of being cooped up in a hotel for nine days. Being in the hotel for three more weeks while we waited for the other home to be finished would have been sheer hell. So, we forfeited our $500 and went for this house. We lived there for eight years. The longest I had ever lived in one place before that was for just more than ten years.

As we unpacked, I was sad to see that so many of our things were ruined. As just one example, the vinyl on my cheap PayLess shoes had simply melted off.

So many members of the Church came to help us unload. They formed a "chain gang" to help us unload our food storage cans, making the job relatively effortless and productive. Like little ants organizing a colony, everything fell together rather quickly.

The kids loved their school, Crippen Elementary; it was named after the astronaut Robert L Crippen. Even though it was just down the street, they still rode the school bus. Zach went there for fifth grade, and the rest of the kids went there until we moved away and I divorced Brad.

We made so many memories there, I don't know where to start. Looking back, they were probably the happiest eight years of my life. We lived in a wonderful neighborhood. I loved going on the zoo field trip with Dani, to the Natural Science Museum with Patrick, and to the farm with Cameron. The kids participated in school plays, programs, parties, and Girl Scouts. We went to the pool after five p.m.—it was shaded then, and my fair-skinned children were protected from sunburn.

I had begun using the tanning beds and also started jogging instead of walking. I was lifting ten-pound weights, and my muscles were showing. Every time Patrick had a friend over, he'd say, "Mom, show them your muscles." He was so proud of me—just as I later was of him when he started working out after we moved.

As usual, I absolutely loved everything about my life except who I was married to. I also felt a huge void that was once filled with the fellowship of AA. I had been going to meetings only about once a year, and I decided to go back. I had nineteen years of sobriety and thought I had my stuff together pretty well. It took about a year to see how I had slowly regressed and was gradually going back to my old ways and spiraling downhill. It was so gradual that I couldn't even see it.

We all got in the "Nana-boat," as Dani called it—a huge, eight-passenger Savannah van with two TVs on which the kids could watch videos. With a little persistence, we located the Alano Club, where I was to make so many good friends.

I also saw many friends pass away, mostly sober. One friend, Linda, was so scared of going to jail for her third DUI that she hung herself in the closet, leaving her two teenage kids and fiancé behind. I first met Linda at another member's house where just six of us AA women were invited for a dinner and meeting. Linda had just gotten out of rehab and seemed high-class. She was so pretty. I envied her; she seemed to have it all.

Janice was another of those six women. She later died from lung cancer at the age of thirty-nine. It's amazing where life takes you along your journey, who you meet, and where you all end up.

Toward the end, Brad ended up resenting all the time I spent away from him, so I had to fight to keep going to my meetings. As I left, he yelled things like, "Why don't you just go live with your freaking AA friends?" after calling me every name in the book loudly enough for all the neighbors to hear. It was a nightmare when I got home each night, but I went anyway. I discovered if we had sex after I came home it seemed to calm his boiling cauldron, so it became an unspoken rule. I could go to a meeting free of any consequence as long as we had sex afterward, or I'd pay dearly. I gave him what he wanted because I was willing to go to any length to be able to go to my AA meetings. I had to be.

I remember often going into the master bathroom, getting on my knees, and pleading with the Lord to help me get through this and to make it go by quickly. Brad had no idea how despicable and appalling he was to me. Since it was always dark when I came home from meetings, I often cried while we had sex. I hated it that much.

Before I started attending live meetings, I joined AAFF, an online AA group. It made my days begin on a bright note and gave me a spiritual high. There I met Keith. I call him my brother, as he is more like a brother to me than my real brother (who still calls me his "late sister"). Keith once posted a story about driving in traffic in Connecticut. A man started incessantly honking at him until Keith got so angry that he poured his hot chocolate from Circle K on the windshield of the guy's car. Imagine how embarrassing it was for him to hear, "Wrong car, jerk." I found many of his posts to be quite comical; others were downright devastating.

He had been in and out of the program like my friend Kevin for twenty years, and he referred to himself as Doubting Thomas. I somehow felt as if God wanted me to instill in him the fact that he could and would get sober and stay that way. We became best friends and talked every single day. I never got emotionally or romantically attached to him, but to avoid confrontation with Brad, Keith wrote to me over the name *Betty Thomas*.

"Betty" wrote me words of encouragement every morning, as she knew what I was going through; I tried to do the same for Keith regarding alcohol. Keith was one of the first people I was able to open up to and talk to about my abuse in a very long time. As I wrote to Keith, my palms got sweaty and I began to get very shaky and full of anxiety, even though Brad was out of town. Just the thought of what he'd do if he found out I had told somebody terrified me. Writing to Keith did make it easier for me to talk in live meetings, and Keith was the person I'd call for a reality check when I could no longer distinguish reality from delusion.

Then one day out of the blue, "Betty" completely stopped writing to me or the rest of the group. My heart sunk. Keith had ended up on the streets of Connecticut and had lost his wallet, his shoes, his belt, his glasses, and his car. He had nothing left. In desperation, his father joined the group to find his friends who might be willing to help. Keith had burned all his bridges in the Connecticut area, and no one would allow him back; he'd been through all the detox and treatment centers many times and owed so much money. The sad thing is, if you don't have insurance, you're out of luck—and most alcoholics or addicts who have hit rock bottom don't even have a job, much less insurance. The ones who need it the most can't get the help they need and so desperately deserve.

I remembered how easy it was for me to get into the Aspire Hotel Alcoholic Treatment Center in Redding, where they offered job training and charged by a sliding scale—if you have no money, you pay no money. So just for the heck of it, I called them to see if they'd take Keith. They said they would as long as they had a bed, and they said he'd have to be drunk to detox.

Keith's dad liked the idea as well, and to our utter surprise, Keith agreed. Now it was just a matter of getting this drunken Keith from Connecticut to California . . . what were the odds it would work? He showed up at his dad's and was desperate for help. His dad made him a care package with meats, cheese and crackers, and other food for the trip—and a bottle of vodka.

All of us in the group were following his progress along the way when suddenly he vanished into thin air. It turns out he almost died. He started bloating up and turning blue and purple, so the bus driver called an ambulance at one of the stops. He was treated at the hospital for alcohol poisoning and got back on the bus at the same stop exactly twenty-four hours later. He ended up throwing his vodka away when he got to Salt Lake City.

He stayed at the treatment center for ninety days, and my mom went from Ukiah to Redding to pick him up—a three-and-a-half-hour drive. Even more miraculously, she and her husband, Gary, allowed him to stay at their house until I was able to escape once again. It took about a month.

Keith and I became roommates and rented a townhouse. The kids and I slept upstairs, and Keith slept downstairs on a cot and air mattress. One day Cameron knocked on the door when we thought he was in his room. To our surprise, he had gotten out of the bedroom window, onto the roof of the van, then somehow to the ground without a scratch. It was funny and utterly terrifying all at once.

My mom asked me once if we'd ever had sex, and I told her no. She said, "Poor guy." *What was she thinking?* She knew I was a member of The church of Jesus Christ of Latter-day Saints, and she knew that the Church asks members to abstain from sexual relations before marriage. She had once been a member of the church herself but had become inactive. Nonetheless, she still knew the standards!

Somehow Brad found out where I was. He sent me flowers; I sent them back. I agreed to go home, and he flew out to get me. But I changed my mind, and he left without me. I finally decided to go back; when he called, I was crying. He asked me what was wrong, and I said I didn't want to go home, yet I *had* to. I had spent a few days packing and unpacking all day long. I'd be so sure I was staying until I'd get almost unpacked, then I'd get scared and start packing up again. That cycle repeated itself over and over and over. It was like an alcoholic fighting off the urge to take a drink then suddenly giving in.

My mom said that normal people don't pack and unpack in a day. If she only knew it had been several times a day and for several days. . . . That's part of the dissociation. I'd forget all the bad, start packing up, get scared, and start unpacking again. It was driving me crazy. I felt like I had a war going on inside my head. It was tremendous agony. I had gone back to smoking and drinking coffee and was a wreck.

Another person I met on my online AA site was Jack. He seemed like he had it all together, yet he had many fewer years of sobriety than I did. He was a good five years older than I was, and I liked that. I asked him to be my sponsor and was surprised when he said yes, especially when AA suggests that people sponsor only those of their same gender.

Jack helped me work through the steps for my second divorce. If not for him, I would never have gotten up the courage to go see a divorce lawyer. I did it all behind Brad's back because I was terrified of what he'd do if he found out.

The day I left for the courthouse, I left my house casually, saying I was going tanning. I had a skirt hidden in my purse and changed while driving out of our cul-de-sac. I thought I was doing the right thing. Jack had already joined the church for me by then, so I thought we were meant to be. Even though my attorney knew Brad had no idea I was divorcing him, when asked by the judge if Brad knew what I was doing, the attorney nodded her head as if to tell me to say yes. So, I did. My attorney knew Brad had no clue, but she also knew he might kill me.

Jack and I developed an emotional connection that I hadn't planned on, and I thought I loved him. After about six times going back and forth between him and Brad, I realized it was the emails that sucked me in, as he had a way with words—but I was in no way even slightly attracted to the physical Jack. Unlike Keith, Jack wasn't the same man in person as he was online. I arranged with my mom to drive the U-Haul to Minnesota, where I was to marry Jack as soon as Brad and I were divorced.

It was disgusting to even kiss Jack, and I sure as heck didn't want to marry him, but my new sponsor who had been in an abusive relationship as well had been coaching Jack. I called her crying, saying I didn't want to get married and that I wanted to go home only to be told I had no home to go to. I was so uncomfortable. I realized later I thought I needed someone to take care of me and the kids and didn't think I could do it myself.

Jack was unable to consummate the marriage, and I called Brad the next morning. He told me that the church was talking about excommunicating me, which was untrue— Jack and I had never met in person until my divorce from Brad was final. Brad convinced me I had done something wrong and once again had no choice. He arrived the next day to load us up.

The first day I was at Jack's house, he was at work and on his computer when another woman started writing to him. I pretended to be Jack for a while then just told her I was Jack's wife. She said she was sorry and had no idea he was married. There were lots of other women he lied to me about as well, but what should I have expected with me in Houston with Brad and Jack not knowing for sure if I'd ever really come back. At one point I realized there could have been more women than I even knew about. Later I found out there were.

I was married to Jack for fourteen months, even though we hardly lived together—we were together only about two months. Basically, I was legally married to Jack and used it as a safety net while I lived with Brad so we could sleep in separate bedrooms. I didn't like either choice but never imagined there would be a third. I don't count Jack as a husband, even though we were married fourteen months; we were never really together, so he was just a deterrent to keep Brad away until I could figure something out. Then he'd suck me back in with his emails; he had such a way with words, with lying and manipulating. I finally realized what a liar he was. Jack had an older daughter named Rebekka, who got along well with my boys. I had no idea the pain and despair I was putting my children through by going back and forth.

One of the times I was headed to court, I left both Dani and Cameron with Jack and Rich overnight while I flew back to Houston to go to court. I landed in Houston at two a.m., picked up my rental car, and drove to the hotel nearest the Montgomery County courthouse. I got a nice room at the Comfort Inn.

As I was wheeling my bag from my car to the room, I noticed something leaking. *Oh no*, I thought, *there goes my apple juice for breakfast*. I made my way to the front desk, continuously watching the flow of fluid seeping out of my suitcase.

I made it to my room. It was so much nicer than I expected, but I had to be in court in just a few hours, so I didn't have time to enjoy anything such as a hot bath or some news on TV. I tried setting the alarm clock and thought I got it right—besides, I didn't want to bother the front desk person at such an early hour.

I sat down and started going through my things in preparation for getting ready the next day to ensure I'd arrive on time. I was shocked as I opened my suitcase: the leaking liquid wasn't my apple juice. It was a can of hairspray. The lid had come off, and the nozzle had pressed against the bottom of my suitcase until the entire can—my only one—was completely empty. I was devastated; *can it get any worse?* I thought. Oh, it did. Much, much worse.

I soon realized the spray had gotten all over the only skirt I had brought to wear to court. It was a polyester skirt with a rayon lining, and it got soaked. I rinsed it then wrung it out then put it by the heater to dry. Since it was mid-summer in Houston, I imagined I was the only one in the hotel using a heater, but I didn't care. I was a nervous wreck, and when I get very emotional, I get chills, so I didn't mind having the heater on. It helped warm me up.

I organized my makeup and other things I would need the following morning and then tried to go to sleep. It never fails, however. When I have only a few hours to sleep and I have something important to do the next day, I have a very hard time falling asleep. I tried and tried until finally, my cell phone rang. It was my attorney's assistant. "Hi, Malia," she said, "I'm just calling to see if you're almost here."

I freaked out and began to cry, knowing how important this day was. I also knew I couldn't possibly drag it out another day with all the expenses it would entail.

I then explained to my attorney's assistant what had happened—how I had gotten only a few hours of sleep and that the hotel alarm clock hadn't gone off and . . . and. . . .

"It's okay," she said; "your attorney isn't even here yet. You still have plenty of time; just get here when you can."

It usually takes me approximately one and a half hours from start to finish to get ready, so I knew I'd need to cut a few corners. I hurried into the shower and washed my hair. *Oh, you've got to be kidding me—no conditioner? What kind of hotel has shampoo but no conditioner? Or at least conditioning shampoo?* I was starting to panic; I couldn't even run a comb through my hair without conditioning it.

I then decided on the worst-case scenario: I grabbed the tiny bottle of hotel lotion and proceeded to run it through my hair with my fingers, smoothing out the knots until I could comb through it. So much for using my curling brush, as my hair would never stay in place anyway without hairspray. I went over to grab my skirt to finish getting ready, and it was standing up by itself—all the hairspray was still in it.

I walked into the courthouse only moments before my attorney, Shauna, got there. No one but Shauna and I knew how late I really was. I'm sure I looked like I had just been run over by a bus with hardly any makeup on due to lack of time. My hair had an oily, greasy sheen from the lotion. And my skirt looked like it had been starched to death. I really was at my worst.

I took a seat quietly in the back. My soon-to-be-ex-husband and my boys were in front of me. I was so embarrassed; I didn't even want him to see me. Before we saw the mediator, the boys took off through the courthouse to hide. I felt so bad for them. I knew they loved me; they just didn't want to move to Minnesota *again*! They had no idea I'd be letting them stay in Texas. Brad had promised to keep them active in the church we attended, which he never did. He also promised to treat them nicely, which wasn't the case either.

Both my attorney and the mediator said this was a stand-in judge they didn't know, so things could go either way; however, they felt I would be granted full custody and Brad would most likely get supervised visitation. He had a history of child abuse against him in the state of Texas. My attorney was just one county from where Andrea Yates had drowned her five children in the bathroom. Her trial was at the same courthouse mine was.

I would have chosen full custody of the kids with Brad getting only supervised visits. After all, I had so much evidence against Brad. But Zach and Patrick both knew I'd be going back to Jack in Minnesota, and they'd had enough moving back and forth—plus, they didn't want to leave their classmates. Brad promised me if I gave him the chance, he would be nicer to them and make sure they kept going to church. He also said he'd allow them to go back to Scouts. So, I let them stay. Later, Brad told the boys they weren't good enough to go to Scouts, and he no longer allowed them to attend.

Brad had also sworn never to lay a hand on either one of them, and he had promised to keep them all active in the church. His word fell through on both counts.

At one point while I was living with Brad but still married to Jack, Brad actually agreed to let me fly out alone to Minnesota to see who I really wanted to be with—him or Jack. He was all mushy and crying and spent more than

$1,000 on my ticket. I'm pretty sure someone else put this thought in Brad's head; I doubt he would have come up with it on his own. It was the Fourth of July, and I was able to look out over Hartford, Connecticut, after my layover and see the fireworks from above.

When Jack picked me up, I was super tired and wanted to go to my hotel room, but he insisted I go to his house for a while. Before I knew it, he had undressed himself. I left and called Brad and arranged to leave the next morning without telling Jack. I went back to Brad instead of staying the three days with Jack as I'd planned.

Back in Houston, Brad did an online divorce between me and Jack. I went to court and I said I didn't want one. Brad eventually found out that I had refused the divorce, and he was furious. This went on and on until finally, I knew I needed to divorce Jack for good—and I'm so glad I did.

The last month Brad and I were together, he had no idea we were divorced, so I had to be exceptionally creative as to how to avoid having sex with him for thirty days. One day while I was unloading the dishwasher, something told me to check the mail. His office was by the front door and windows, and he always got the mail, but I stopped everything and went. It turned out his copy of the divorce papers was in the mail that day. I hid it.

I found an online job. I figured I would have to support myself and my children one day, and I loved working for this online call center.

After the divorce from Jack—fourteen months from the day we married—our bishop remarried me and Brad. I went into the bathroom and cried while he was on his way. About a year later, I was able to face Brad about wanting a divorce. Somehow, maybe because our entire church congregation knew, he complied. He even helped me move into a three-bedroom, two-bath townhouse I really loved and could afford. Zach and Patrick decided they had moved enough, and they opted to stay with their dad.

CHAPTER TEN

Martin Luther King Jr. said, "Our lives begin to end the day we become silent about the things that matter." My life with Brad was living proof of the truth of that statement.

I'll never forget the time I picked Zach up from his friend's house. Once we got home, Brad got mad at him for something. I was in our bedroom and could hear loud thumping all the way down the hall from his room. As I was walking out of our room, Brad walked out of Zach's room and, for the first time, actually admitted it. "I beat him," he said; "I lost it and I beat him."

Just hearing his voice made my skin crawl. I ran back into the master bedroom and quickly dialed 911. I let it ring twice and then hung up, knowing that if Brad heard me calling, I'd be in huge trouble. I was so hoping they would send help after tracing where the call originated from. All calls to 911 from our house were a real emergency, as we never knew when the hot lava underneath the volcano would erupt, spewing rocks and boulders in all directions.

By then Brad had gone downstairs, so I went into Zach's room. Zach was curled up on his bed with his arms holding his legs near him in a fetal position. When the officers finally arrived, I believed justice would finally prevail. I was asked to come out and speak with one of the officers and tell him my side of the story as the other officer went inside Zach's room to talk with him.

I fully expected Brad to be handcuffed and hauled off to jail, which was where I felt he belonged. My heart was leaping with joy at the very thought of it. Not once had he ever faced the consequences of any harm he had ever done to me or the children. This time, though, his anger and rage and abuse of Zach were so bad that he freely admitted what he had done. Surely this time justice would be served.

After talking to the officer, I walked back into Zach's room; his eyes were wide as saucers, and he was scared to death. The officer told me Zach said he was okay—and the officer said he could find no visible marks. *Of course, you can't, you stupid idiot,* I spat out in my own mind, *how could anyone see anything beneath that mop of hair?* I was disgusted with the officer. I was crushed when the officers left; Brad got away with hurting one of my babies once again. He didn't even get a slap on the hand.

On another occasion, Zach, Patrick, and I were out in the kitchen when Brad got mad over something. It could have been anything, since he so easily got set off by the tiniest of things. Brad smacked Zach around, pushing him to the ground. Then Brad grabbed Zach by the neck and squeezed as he raised his other fist, getting ready to punch Zach right in the face.

I screamed, which startled Brad enough to make him stop. Then I grabbed the phone to call 911. Brad pulled the phone out of my hands after I had dialed only the first two digits and then threw it across the floor with such force that he broke it. The phone was no longer usable.

I later reported the incident, but nothing was ever done. Brad should have at least been charged with interfering with a 911 call.

I wanted to be able to take care of my kids on my own but had never lived alone and taking care of them and myself seemed unsurmountable. I once checked myself and my two youngest children into the women's shelter. My older boys never would have come. Since I was vegetarian, most of my meals were peanut butter and jelly sandwiches. I was getting homesick. I gave Dani and Cameron a bath, and we walked into the cafeteria for a snack. They both had white socks on. By the time we had gotten back to our room, the soles of their socks were pitch black. I missed the cleanness we once lived in.

The shelter had given Dani and Cameron clothes, and it was about time to start school. All the kids were to meet out front and go from there. Everything was so foreign; I wanted what we once had. The peace of having my own home over-whelmed me, and I forgot all the bad. I finally broke down and went back to the comforts we had, even if it meant putting up with a devil. After all, I reasoned, he wasn't always so bad, and it would be worth it. Sadly, that wasn't the case; the abuse continued to escalate and get worse for my children.

Once we were all in our master bedroom, and Brad grabbed my cell phone and broke it with his bare hands in front of me and all the kids. Zach then ran downstairs and out the back door. Brad quickly grabbed the keys to my Tahoe so I couldn't leave, then grabbed the cordless phone and took it with him as he went running after Zach down the trails behind the homes in our cul-de-sac. Zach was faster than Brad, so he got away, and quickly. With Brad having the cordless phone and my car keys, I was trapped. I was being held hostage in my own home, and I couldn't leave or even call for help.

Once Brad told Zach to get out of the house, meaning he wanted Zach to leave permanently. Poor Zach was just twelve years old. He walked out the back door and walked a couple of miles to his friend's house. His friend wasn't home. He had nowhere else to go, so he came back home. It was a hot summer day, and his tender, bare feet got blisters from walking so far on the hot pavement.

Once when the boys were getting ready to go to Scouts at our church, I heard Brad yelling, "I'm going to knock your teeth down your throat!" Brad suddenly picked Patrick up and threw him across the room. Thank goodness he landed in my recliner chair; it flipped over, and he rolled out of it, completely unharmed but visibly shaken to the core. His wide, baby-blue eyes were filled with both fear and disbelief.

Next to Zach, Dani was Brad's second-favorite target. One day she kept running around our huge dining room table. He yelled at me to stop her so he could spank her, but no way was I going to enable his abuse; I was already enabling it enough by continuing to live in the same house with him.

Dani turned and ran up the stairs. She made it to the landing before he was able to grab onto some part of her body and drag her back down, leaving a good-sized bruise on her arm.

I later took her into our bathroom to take pictures while pretending I was just bathing her. I thought having photos would surely result in justice—they were visible proof. I saved the photo for the upcoming divorce; however, we ended up settling out of court, so the picture was never seen by anyone other than my attorney.

One day I was leaving the women's shelter after getting some questions answered, and by the time I got back out to my car, thirty minutes later, I had about twenty missed calls from Brad. I panicked; I couldn't let him know what I had been doing. I drove to where I go to get my hair done and asked the girl to just wash my hair, nothing more. I got home and told Brad I had gotten a haircut. By then he had already pulled all the kids out of school thinking I was planning another getaway and would get to the kids before he did. By then he was paranoid.

Once I was backing out of our garage to go to an AA meeting, and I accidentally ran over one of the boys' bikes. I ran into the house to tell Brad; the bike was stuck under the Tahoe. He came out yelling and swearing at both the boys without even knowing whose bike it was. Then he climbed under the back of the Tahoe to pull the bike out. My thoughts came in rapid succession: *bike under the car, husband with bike, car door open, Tahoe running, PERFECT!* Yet something stopped me from following through with my desire to run Brad over and end it all. He wasn't worth losing my kids and going to prison for.

Another time the boys were about nine and eleven years old. Brad was yelling and threatening to beat their faces in. It was typical for him. He screamed and yelled at them while calling them horrible names, letting them know how bad he thought they were. He even smacked them around a bit, then suddenly flip-flopped and became Mr. Nice Guy, taking them somewhere special or buying them something—making sure they knew they didn't deserve it to prove what a good dad he really was. Through behavior like that, they became even more loyal and caring to their dad.

We were not allowed to have too much fun. If he ever caught us laughing and having a good time, he was sure to put an end to it using whatever tactic he saw fit at the time. He was miserable, so he wanted to make sure everyone around him was miserable as well—and he did a pretty good job of it. He was truly a curmudgeon.

One Christmas Eve it was a warm evening, and it started to rain. I got a crazy idea to go for a bike ride in the rain, and Patrick came with me. Brad wasn't too keen on the idea, especially when we got back and he saw what a wonderful, fun-filled time we'd had, just being crazy and riding our bikes in the rain.

He was extremely controlling, too. I was not allowed to watch CNN for news—only FOX. He once came downstairs as I was jogging on my treadmill with my headset on listening to music and watching CNN. Brad was filled with disgust and anger, and he immediately changed the channel.

I changed it back as soon as I knew he was gone. He hated Democrats and called them—or everyone else who wasn't a Republican—the most disgusting names imaginable.

Dinnertime was always stressful with just the three girls. I always had a knot in the pit of my stomach that kept me from eating much, which was fine by me. I always preferred the skinny look. Dinnertime was more of a debate tournament in which Brad was always right. He had a big ego coupled with an inferiority complex. He liked to drive big trucks and was not even six feet tall. He had what I called "little man, big truck syndrome."

Once Brad picked Zach up by his shirt so roughly that he left a bruise on Zach's chest. When he saw the bruise, he knew he had gone overboard and had to leave, so he went to Walmart to get away. I had already called 911, and by the time the police arrived, Brad was already gone. I didn't want Brad to know I was the one who had called, so I made the call anonymously and told them to make sure that whoever came would check my children for marks; I wanted to be sure they found the bruise on Zach. Instead, a female sheriff came and said as long as he didn't need medical attention, it was not considered abuse. She said that was just the way some people parent, and she refused to even look at or speak to my children.

As mentioned, we were a county over from Harris County, where the laws were much stricter; had we lived there, he would have wound up in jail multiple times. But since we lived in Montgomery County, the authorities didn't ever seem to want to get involved, and so they didn't. My attorney was appalled.

One day I was leaving the temple to go home. The temple is a place where you are supposed to be able to leave your worldly cares behind while you bask in the presence of the Lord. But how could I not think of all the dysfunction that had been going on in our family's lives for years? I had to wonder if anyone could truly find peace inside that magnificently structured building. Its beauty and architectural work were enough to draw anyone near, but was it possible to find peace?

I decided I'd better call Brad, as I had decided to stop by the blood bank and donate, as we both did regularly. If I didn't call him to report the delay and my whereabouts, my phone would be blasted with calls and messages asking me where I was, making baseless accusations, and telling me I should have been home hours ago.

The knot grew bigger inside my stomach as I pressed the numbers on my phone. "What?" he shouted when he answered. After I explained my situation, he said, "Oh, now you're really being selfish."

Astonished, I thought to myself, *How can giving the gift of life be selfish?* My being away had always bothered him; the second I left the house I could visualize an hourglass filled with sand being turned over. Each speck of sand moved faster than I could ever go. As I felt the panic rise, I said a silent prayer. It didn't seem to help. Was God even listening? Did He even care? After all, it was me—the girl who grew up with the "fat, ugly, and stupid syndrome," never being good enough to please anyone.

I argued with him, which was a rarity, but I felt a little courage because over the phone we had distance between us. He finally permitted me to go donate blood. A cold sweat broke out over my body, and I felt my clothing clinging to me. My sweaty palms were shaking as I walked into the interview room and was left alone to answer some questions on the new computer system they had just installed. Question after question, my mind raced frantically so I could hurry and get out of there and get home just as quickly as I could.

Do you trade sex for drugs? No. Do you trade sex for money? No. Do you trade sex to be able to go to your AA meetings? Darn it, I knew the question had to be there somewhere. My mind could no longer differentiate reality from total dysfunction, chaos, and destruction—what was okay and what wasn't. I knew I was not only a recovering alcoholic, but I no longer had control over my own mind anymore and living the reality of sheer torment felt normal. It was what I was used to and all I knew. I finished the questions, donated blood, and hurried home.

After getting dinner over with and the kids ready for bed, things had calmed down a bit and I boldly announced, "I'm going to an AA meeting."

"Fine," he said, "why don't you just go live with your freaking AA friends? Those meetings aren't making you any better—they're making you worse." He knew I was getting stronger, and he was losing his grip on me—the strangling, suffocating grasp he held onto me with for so many years. He had *schadenfreude* in his blood; God forbid anyone around him should be happy.

Brad had no idea how many times I prayed for his death whenever he had to leave town. I prayed for his plane to crash; I knew that was wrong, but I didn't care. I later thought of all the people who would die along with him, so I changed my prayer to ask that if there was a plane that was going to crash, he would be on it. I knew he had a history of blood clots after his car accident several years earlier, so I also began to pray he'd get a blood clot—fast, painless, over with, and done.

While Brad was once coming home from a long flight, the plane had to circle the tarmac for quite some time before it could move into position. He was in a bad situation. It had been a long flight, and he was a rather large man who had stayed seated a bit too long. Later that night he got a severe pain in his side that landed him in the emergency room. It was a blood clot, all right. Every time I begrudgingly went to visit him and found he was doing okay, my heart sank just a little deeper. I wanted him to die.

During the five-hour waiting period before he was seen, his foot swelled tremendously and turned purple, later leaving him with "drop foot." He later had a fasciotomy, as his leg swelled up so much they had to slice it open so it wouldn't burst. He was in the intensive care unit for two months with a vacuum machine sucking all the ooze out, allowing it to drain. Later he was sent home with a nurse who came daily to change the dressing on his wounds. They wanted to teach me how to do it, but I about passed out every time one of the kids lost a tooth and I saw blood.

I later developed compassion for this man as I cared for him day and night doing absolutely everything for him; he was like an infant, unable to do anything for himself. He later looked like a patchwork quilt as they took skin from his good leg in the shapes of squares and triangles to graft it to his wounds. I knew we could no longer remain in this marriage, but at the same time, God took away the devastating fear I once had toward him. When the time came, I was able to leave after eight failed attempts fleeing for my life while he was gone. I was packing in front of him; he told me he was going to come and kill me and my new husband in bed one night. I kept packing.

Today he is disabled and in a wheelchair. When he does walk, he uses a cane or a walker. How could I possibly go on hating him? The way he was raised had made him the way he was, and it was time to end the cycle of abuse. Then I suddenly realized God *had* been listening. He *did* answer my prayers, just not in the way I had expected. Today we can talk and have a civil conversation—well, most days, that is. I no longer wish for his death but truly want him to be happy.

CHAPTER ELEVEN

When it comes to domestic violence, no one is exempt. I'd like to share several examples that should establish the need to exercise caution.

Once after an AA meeting, a woman came to the club. This particular club was located down a long road that was not heavily traveled. When she arrived, she hadn't eaten and was hungry; luckily, we had a microwave and a well-stocked refrigerator anyone could use. I found enough food in it to make her a decent meal. She was also out of cigarettes. I had quit smoking but gave her some of my nicotine gum, which helped calm her nerves.

As we visited, I learned she was escaping from her husband, who was actively trying to kill her at that very moment. She was shaking and in tears and had bruises all over her arms; the outer cover of half of her car had been torn off where her husband had beat it with a shovel. Now, she said, he was after her.

She asked me for a couple of dollars for gas, but I had no money. A great guy in the program gave me ten dollars and told me to take her to the gas station at the end of the street and make sure she used the money for gas.

I took her to the gas station to fill up. She told me she was heading back to the women's shelter and kept looking around nervously. She said she was afraid for me to follow her there—if her husband found us, she said, chances were good he'd turn on me as well. But I wasn't afraid of him. I was hoping he'd run into us so I could run him over with my Tahoe. We didn't see him along the way back to the women's shelter, and I made sure she was safely inside the shelter before I left.

Then I found out he was one of the scariest kinds of abusers of all. He was a Texas policeman. Cops can often be abusive because they are in a position of authority and power, and the control goes to their heads as they try to dominate their partners.

Domestic violence takes place in a staggering 40 percent of law-enforcement families, but police departments mostly ignore the problem or let it slide. The following excerpt is adapted from *Police Wife: The Secret Epidemic of Police Domestic Violence*, written by ex-police wife Susanna Hope and award-winning investigative journalist Alex Roslin, published as part of the Ms. Blog's Domestic Violence Awareness Month series:

> In 2009, in Utica, New York, police Investigator Joseph Longo Jr. killed his estranged wife, Kristin Palumbo-Longo, stabbing her more than a dozen times in their home, then

stabbed himself to death. One of the couple's four children discovered the horrifying scene on coming home from school that afternoon.

Utica's then-Police Chief Daniel LaBella said the killing was completely unexpected—an incident "no one could have prevented or predicted." But Kristin's family filed a $100-million wrongful-death suit saying city and police officials didn't do enough about Longo's troubling behavior before the tragedy.

Kristin had contacted police at least five times in the weeks before she was murdered, saying she feared her husband might kill her and their kids, but police supervisors discouraged her from making reports or seeking a protection order, the lawsuit said. In a preliminary ruling, a federal judge agreed that the police actions may have "enhanced the danger to Kristin and amounted to deliberate indifference." The city settled the suit in 2013, paying the couple's children $2 million.

The murder wasn't an isolated tragedy. It was unusual only as it was so public and so bloody. A staggering amount of domestic violence rages behind the walls of cops' homes, while most police departments do little about it. In the vast majority of cases, cops who hurt a family member do so in utter secrecy, while their victims live in desperate isolation with very little hope of help. Research shows:

An astonishing 40 percent of cops acknowledged in one U.S. survey that they were violent with their spouse or children in the previous six months.

A second survey had remarkably similar results—40 percent of officers admitted there was violence in their relationship in the previous year. The abuse rate for cops is up to 15 times higher than among the public.

Police discipline is startlingly lax. The LAPD disciplines cops with a sustained domestic violence complaint less strictly than those who lie or get in an off-duty fight. In the Puerto Rico Police Department, 86 percent of cops remained on active duty even after two or more arrests for domestic violence.

It seems incredible that a crime wave of such magnitude and far-reaching social ramifications could be so unknown to the public and yet at the same time an open secret in a mostly indifferent law enforcement community. It is surely one of the most surreal crime epidemics ever—at once disavowed, generalized, and virtually unchecked.

Aptly summing up the bizarre disconnect, retired Lieutenant Detective Mark Wynn of the Nashville Metropolitan Police Department in Tennessee told PBS in a 2013 story on the issue: "What's amazing to me is we're having this conversation at all. I mean, could you imagine us sitting here talking about this and saying, how do you feel about officers using crack before they go to work, or how do you feel about the officer who every once in a while just robs a bank, or every once in a while decides to go in and steal a car from a dealership? We wouldn't have this conversation. Why is it that we've taken violence against women and separated that from other crimes?"

Domestic violence is bad enough for any woman to deal with. Shelters, many of them chronically underfunded, regularly turn away abused women because they're full, while only about one in four incidents in the wider population ever get reported to the police. Hundreds of U.S. communities have adopted "nuisance property" laws that encourage police to pressure landlords to evict tenants who repeatedly call 911 over domestic abuse, further dissuading victims from seeking help.

But abuse at home is far worse for the wife or girlfriend of a cop. Who will she call—911? What if a coworker or friend of her husband responds? Police officers are trained in the use of physical force and know how to hurt someone without leaving a trace.

They have guns and often bring them home. And if a cop's wife runs, where will she hide? He usually knows where the women's shelters are. Some shelter staff admit they are powerless to protect an abused police spouse. Her abuser may have training and tools to track her web use, phone calls, and travels to find out if she is researching how to get help or, if she has fled, where she went.

In the rare case where the woman works up the nerve to complain, the police department and justice system often victimize her again. She must take on the infamous blue wall of silence—the strict unwritten code of cops protecting each other in investigations. The police have a name for it—extending "professional courtesy." In the words of Anthony Bouza, a one-time commander in the New York Police Department and former police chief of Minneapolis, "The Mafia never enforced its code of blood-sworn omerta with the ferocity, efficacy and enthusiasm the police bring to the Blue Code of Silence."

It all adds up to the police having a de facto license to abuse their spouses and children. And it's a worldwide phenomenon that police families struggle with everywhere from Montreal to Los Angeles, Puerto Rico, the U.K., Australia, and South Africa.

The torrent of abuse is virtually unknown to the public, but without realizing it, we all pay a steep price. Domestic violence is the single most common reason the public contacts the police in the U.S., accounting for up to 50 percent of all calls in some areas. Yet, a battered woman who calls 911 may have a two-in-five chance of an abuser coming to her door. Official investigations have found law enforcement departments that tolerate abuse in police homes also mishandle violence against women in other homes.

Abusive cops are also more prone to other forms of misconduct on the job—such as brutality against civilians and violence against fellow officers. We all pay as taxpayers when governments have to settle multi-million-dollar lawsuits with victims of police abuse or negligence. Police domestic violence also has close connections to a host of other problems—police killings of African Americans, sexual harassment of female drivers at traffic stops and women cops, and even more broadly, issues like growing social inequality and subjugation of Native Americans.

And police officers themselves are victims, too. Even though our society calls cops heroes, we give them little support to cope with the pressure of police work. A big part of the job is to wield power to control other people. As a result, policing attracts people who are good at controlling others or may have a craving for that kind of power—and then trains them to use their power better. Control is also the main driver of domestic violence. Is it a surprise then that so many cops are violent at home?

Susanna Hope (a pseudonym for security and privacy reasons) is a Canadian professional writer who was married for over 20 years to a police officer. She has two sons and two grandchildren.

Alex Roslin is an award-winning Canadian journalist who was president of the board of the Canadian Centre for Investigative Reporting. His investigative and writing awards include three Canadian Association of Journalists prizes for investigative reporting, a gold prize in the National Magazine Awards, and nine nominations for CAJ awards and NMAs.

I got carpel tunnel syndrome during each of my pregnancies, and sometimes it lasted a while after I delivered the baby. I was told it can also go away on its own or that in some cases it can get worse and require surgery. It was bothering me at a particular time while we were living in Houston, and due to a glamorous, heartwarming commercial, I came very close to going to the Brown Hand Center. However, you cannot use appearances as a gauge: a violent person can appear charming and hide it very well. It reminds me of the old saying, "Never judge a book by its cover." I share the following as an example of what can happen—and as a warning to be extremely careful about trusting even seemingly impressive professionals without doing your own research.

Michael Brown was born in Galena Park in the greater Houston area. He attended Galena Park Junior High School, where he saw a film of Michael DeBakey performing heart surgery. He wanted to be a heart surgeon, but he said that he ultimately became a hand surgeon because the specialty allowed for greater creativity and was "more profitable and glamorous."

He graduated from Galena Park High School with honors in 1975 and attended the Southwest Texas State University (now Texas State University-San Marcos), where he received a grade point average of 3.97. He then graduated from the Baylor College of Medicine. He received his medical license in 1983 and did surgical training in a hospital in Stockton, California.

Brown founded the Brown Hand Center in 1988. He also owned, managed, or was an officer in several other medical businesses, including the St. Michael's Center for Specialty Surgery with locations in three states; the Achilles Foot and Ankle Specialists, LLC; and the Allied Center for Special Surgery.

He became well-known in Houston for television advertisements showing him with Sophie, his baby daughter; the ads ended with the slogan, "In the Brown Hand Center, we'll

care for you just as I care for my own family." The same
advertisements also aired in the greater Phoenix area. This
commercial showed his most charming side, and having his
family beside him made it all look even more precious. (The
actual commercials are still available on the internet.)

Brown was making $2.5 million annually by the early
twenty-first century. He had a mansion in the Memorial area
of Houston as well as a residence in the East Wedgwood Glen
section of The Woodlands, an upper-scale neighborhood. At
his death in 2013, he also owned a mansion in Miami Beach,
Florida; a ranch in Normangee; and a residence in New York.
As of 2010, the Brown Hand Center had locations in Houston, Dallas, Austin, Las Vegas, and Phoenix, and Brown's
businesses were expected to gross about $45 million in the
next year, more than in the previous five years.

Michael Brown was also prominent in Houston society.
In 2008, despite being already involved in scandals, he was
awarded the Republican Congressional Medal of Distinction;
in connection with the award, he had dinner with President
George W. Bush and lunch with Vice President Dick Cheney.
In 2010, he threw the first pitch at a Houston Astros game.

Michael Brown advertised the "patented Brown technique" of carpal tunnel surgery, endoscopic surgery for the
wrist; the Brown Hand Center advertisements and website
credited him with inventing the technique and contrasted it
with more traditional surgery, which requires stitches. But
in 2010, Dr. Robert Szabo, the president of the American
Society for Surgery of the Hand and the chief hand surgeon
of the University of California-Davis School of Medicine,

told Todd Ackermann of the *Houston Chronicle* that Brown's business had "nothing unique . . . in regard to the surgeries they perform or helping hand patients generally." According to Szabo and other orthopedic surgeons, Brown's claim to a special technique rested on his having patented his own surgical instruments, which resembled those used by other hand surgeons.

Michael Brown was married four times. In 2002, he was convicted of beating his third wife and was placed on probation by the Texas Medical Board for that and for "concerns he had an alcohol or chemical dependency." In 2006, after Brown tested positive for cocaine, the Board revoked his license to practice medicine. As of 2010, advertising for the Brown Hand Center promoted Michael Brown's medical background, mentioned his medical degree, and stated that he was retired but trained the doctors who worked at the centers. Seth Chandler, a University of Houston professor of law, called the ads "misleading" but "[not] a slam dunk for anyone looking to prosecute" under the Texas Medical Practice Act.

In August 2010, Michael Brown voluntarily forfeited parental rights to his two children by his third wife; in September 2011, after a week-long trial, he was acquitted of felony assault on his fourth wife.

The revenues of the Brown Hand Center decreased after advertisements featuring Brown ended circulation. Brown moved to the greater Miami area, and on January 23, 2013, filed a Chapter 11 bankruptcy petition in the United States Bankruptcy Court for the Southern District of Florida. The case was transferred to the U.S. Bankruptcy Court in Houston on September 25, 2013, and the appointment of a Trustee was approved on September 30. A restructuring officer was named for Michael Brown's businesses in March.

In July 2013, Michael Brown pleaded guilty in federal court to interfering with a flight attendant. He was sentenced to thirty days in federal jail on September 25 and was ordered to surrender himself on October 25 of that same year.

The Brown Hand Center announced it was closing in October 2013. Only the Houston location remained open by October 16. The trustee handling Brown's bankruptcy case had placed the business in Chapter 11 protection; he stated that he had discovered "significant financial debt, misuse of revenue, and compliance issues."

The news was released that Brown had been found unconscious at his house in Miami Beach on October 29, 2013. His attorneys filed a statement with the U.S. Bankruptcy Court confirming that he had suffered cardiac arrest and was incapacitated: "Dr. Brown remains hospitalized. . . . It appeared to be severe and, at that time, counsel cannot communicate with Dr. Brown. The extent of the damage he has suffered was unknown." Five days earlier—on October 24, 2013—he had been found with a suicide note.

At that time Michael Brown was taken to the Mount Sinai Medical Center & Miami Heart Institute in Miami Beach, where on November 7 he was declared brain dead. According to Dick Guerin, his attorney, life support was removed; he died the following day at the age of fifty-six.

Before his death, several of Michael Brown's assets—including briefcases containing $3.2 million in cash, art and antiques, and a $250,000 item of jewelry—were reported missing and unaccounted for. After his death, a series of auctions of his possessions were held to pay debts.

I almost went to Dr. Michael Brown because his commercials were so appealing. Luckily, my carpal tunnel ended up going away for the most part, so I never had to deal with surgery of any kind.

So, here you have a cop and a brilliant doctor—neither of whom you would expect to commit domestic violence. Just remember: Men who commit domestic violence can often be sociopaths, can be experts at mind control, and can look absolutely charming from the outside—someone you would never expect.

If anyone tells you she is being abused, believe her—no matter how "normal" or even charming the alleged abuser appears. Women don't make up allegations of abuse to get attention or to get the man in trouble; 99.9 percent of the time it's the truth.

We often hear, "He looked so nice," "He was such a nice guy," "I never would have expected," and other similar sentiments. It's time we all wake up and expect the unexpected, because domestic violence is much more rampant than we ever could have realized.

Take a look at the findings. According to an article published in the *Houston Chronicle*, in the United States, 10 to 35 percent of the population will be physically aggressive toward a partner at some point in their lives. Nearly 60 percent of all young women have experienced abuse; 29 percent of women surveyed said they'd been in an abusive relationship, and 62 percent of those women have been hit, shoved, or slapped. Yet according to some studies, fewer than 1 percent of domestic violence cases are reported to the police.

According to the *Chronicle*, domestic violence is now commonly defined broadly to include "all acts of physical, sexual, psychological or economic violence" that may be committed by a family member or intimate partner. "Family violence is a broader term, often used to include child abuse, elder abuse, and other violent acts between family members."

CHAPTER TWELVE

When I found my soulmate online, I wasn't actually looking. In fact, I told *everyone* after my divorce from Brad that I wasn't going to get into a relationship for at least one year. I knew how bad my track record was for picking the wrong kind of guy, every time!

I worked for an online call center from home, and one day while I was in my apartment after the divorce, I heard a still, small voice tell me to Google the online dating site, LDS Singles. I've learned over the years to know when a thought is from me or God. This certainly wasn't my plan. So, I did as directed, and I found Scott.

Scott had joined and signed up for six months. He had only seventeen days left on his membership. He was forty-five, so he put himself in the age group for forty-five and under. I am ten months older than he is, so I put myself in the forty-six to fifty group. Had *I* not found *him*, he never would have seen my profile.

It's not this way in the live world, but so many guys from LDS Singles wanted to call me or email me; in fact, I was corresponding with so many different men I forgot what I had said to which one. There are a lot of desperate guys out there. It got ridiculous, so, I decided to narrow it down to three. Scott was one of those.

I initially started writing to Scott, but then I chose another guy who was an ex-cop. I had been corresponding with my bishop in Redding, and he advised me to be careful, saying that cops can sometimes be abusive. The bishop's message came to my inbox three times. I asked him if he had sent it three times, and he said he hadn't. That was a *big* red flag letting me know the ex-cop was not the one.

So, I went back to Scott and one other man in whom I wasn't too interested. Because of my earlier "false start," Scott almost said no thanks.

My divorce from Brad was final in June 2009. I met Scott online in July 2009. We got engaged the day we met in person in October and were married on January 1, 2010.

My older boys wanted to stay with their dad so they could be with their friends, so I packed up and took my two youngest kids, Dani and Cameron, to live with Scott in Utah. Scott had five kids; four were living at home, but one went on a mission right after we got married.

My online job was transferable wherever I went, so I had a job waiting when I got to Utah. One day I failed to read the closing page of a sale verbatim, and I was fired. I then found a job at Occurrence; it was the first and only real job I ever had outside the home, and I loved it. I was there for almost five years.

Once Patrick got sick, I went back and forth to Houston for about a week at a time. Though Patrick and Zach were supposed to come to Utah every other summer, Brad refused to let them come; they were finally allowed to visit only once, just four months before Patrick got sick. Four months later, Patrick died from cancer at the age of seventeen. I was blessed that my job allowed me so much time off that I was able to be with him about half the time he was in the hospital, which was seventy-seven days. (My mom died two years later in her sleep of an opioid overdose at the age of seventy-seven; too many seventy-sevens!)

My mom was the first to buy *Just Don't Forget Me*, the book I wrote for Patrick, and she sent one to my niece and one to my brother. I then found her and my brother bashing my book on Facebook. I was simply a grieving mother, and maybe I didn't know quite how to write a book—but I think maybe, just maybe, she was just jealous that I had accomplished something she never could have. Then she went on Amazon and wrote a horrible review about how I focused more on myself, which took the spotlight off my son; I guess she didn't understand that it was written in a biographical format, with cancer being a secondary subject. I think she was just evil, and to be honest, I haven't missed her at all.

About two years after living with his dad, and one and a half years before Patrick got sick, he wrote this on his Facebook wall:

> *October 26, 2011*
> *I hope you'll all remember me well. As*
> *a good friend, as a nice guy, or just as the*
> *kid who made you laugh, I love all you guys.*
> *Even the random people I just click "accept"*

because we have some mutual friends. I'm not going to be around forever, and I just want you all to know that you're awesome. I don't know if there is a God, or what he has in store for me, but the way things have been going so far, he doesn't seem to like me too much. I'll stick around for all of you guys, and in return, just don't forget me. . . .

(The book I wrote in Patrick's honor was inspired by that Facebook post. You can still find it on Amazon published in 2015.)

When Patrick first got sick, Brad took him to the hospital, and they said he had the flu. He wanted to become a marine biologist, so even though he was getting progressively sicker, it was important for him to take the TAX test in Texas. The school arranged for another student to push him around in a wheelchair for half a day for three days. On the first day, he developed a fever and his blood pressure dropped. They called Brad, who said he would meet them at the emergency room. He then ended up at Texas Children's Hospital in Houston, where he stayed for seventy-seven days before he died from HLH and T-cell lymphoma.

I'll never forget the moment I walked in and Patrick was hooked up to life support. I couldn't get close due to the tubes coming out of his neck. The nurse noticed my anguish and motioned for me to come around to the other side. Patrick gestured for his cell phone, but his right hand wasn't working well because a nerve had been nicked during surgery.

He then grabbed a stack of pictures, turning them over and going through them all until he found a picture of a heart. He pointed to it as a tear rolled down his cheek. I asked, "Are you trying to tell me that you love me?" He nodded yes. I was heartbroken to see my poor baby boy this way.

His best friend had told me that once as he went to visit Patrick, Brad had smacked Patrick hard in the face, leaving a mark and giving him a bloody nose. I was furious and remembered a text Patrick sent saying, "Mom, Dad's being really mean to me." By the time I saw the text and responded to Patrick, everything was fine, so I didn't pry.

I later learned Brad bought him a salt-water aquarium. He couldn't wait for me to see it. He loved sea slugs, and his favorite was a beautiful bright-blue one with black on it. As no one knew how to take care of the water properly, everything in the aquarium died one by one. It was so sad.

The day I went to the hospital, I must have looked like a madwoman. I told the front desk people to get Brad out of there—that I had a right to see my son alone. I told them that if they didn't, I was going to scratch Brad's eyes out. They took me seriously, so Patrick and I did finally have some privacy for a short time.

I stayed at a motel and went back and forth to downtown Houston, about a forty-five-minute drive, to see him every day at the Texas Children's Hospital. I also paid for both my oldest daughters to fly to Houston, and I paid for all their food and a room for them for a week. I kept easy-to-make food in my room and ate a lot of peanut-butter-and-jelly sandwiches, which were always available and free in the lunchroom.

I was on Facebook one day and heard the song by Kansas, "Carry On, Wayward Son." The lyrics saying that heaven was waiting reminded me of Patrick, and at that very moment, I just *knew* he was going to die. Even toward the end of that day as they were planning the date for his release from the hospital, I knew.

I remember my very last day. It was the end of my week-long vacation; my rental car was loaded and ready to go. Patrick and I had had a wonderful last day together. His fever had come back, and he was feeling exhausted, but the doctors were optimistic. They had asked me to stay longer once before, but they didn't this time. I said goodbye to Patrick and hugged him tightly, knowing it was for the last time. We both said our goodbyes, and as I stood at the door, I turned around to get one last look. He cleared his throat and said, "Goodbye, Mom, I love you." He died the next morning.

I'm so grateful I was able to talk to him on the phone the morning he died, even though he couldn't speak back to me. First, they said he wouldn't make it through the day, then the hour, then ten minutes, then he was just gone.

A part of me died with him. I had started walking to keep in shape when I quit smoking in 1987; my walks turned into jogging, then almost three hours daily at the gym. Once Patrick died, I completely stopped everything for almost five years. My hair began to fall out and all but about three inches broke off, so I started wearing wigs. I still wear them to church and on special occasions. I love my wigs so much more than my real hair.

Because I had been getting so many perms and highlights, I was told my hair was too damaged and I could only do one or the other. I chose highlights, as I'm getting a touch of grey. To my surprise, the straight, thin, fine hair I'd had my entire life grew back in curly and is still that way today. Someone told me that was Patrick's gift to me since I could no longer get perms.

I am so glad Patrick went home to his Heavenly Father rather than his earthly father, because I know he will never again be abused. I also know he's free from pain and sorrow and is in a happy place. I can't wait to see him again.

We'll never forget Patrick. We still celebrate his birthday by having cheesecake; his favorite was raspberry. We set a place for him at Christmas and on Thanksgiving. For Thanksgiving dinner, we pile all the food and desserts you can imagine—including rolls—on paper plates and go driving around until we find a homeless person who hasn't eaten. That is Patrick's gift to them, and it has become our family tradition.

Since Patrick wanted to become a marine biologist, we had him buried at sea a one-hour boat ride offshore from Galveston Island. First, he was cremated. He was then placed in a biodegradable bag designed to sink to the ocean floor and later become part of the coral reef. It was his eighteenth birthday.

On the way there, I didn't see a single bird; however, on the way back, the boat was swarmed with dozens of seagulls for about half an hour. It was pretty amazing. Now whenever I see a seagull, it reminds me of Patrick.

We originally wanted to take him to a place called "The Flower Garden," but it was a five-hour boat ride both ways, so we decided on the site that was only an hour away. Many of Patrick's friends were there with their siblings and their parents; I didn't even know some of them. Among the group that gathered to mourn him were two of his favorite teachers, a few more parents, and our family. It was the last time our entire family—me and my six children—would all be together.

I remember one of Brad's friends holding the small, tan box, which held all that was left of what used to be my son. My mind could not comprehend such a thing. I didn't want to even touch it. It wasn't my son!

We all met on the pier, and the captain chose the spot. She thought Patrick might like a place where there was a sunken ship. It was a pleasant, sunny day as we boarded the *Texsun II*.

It was a medium-sized boat that could hold as many as 150 people. It had a deck where people could walk around and a cabin underneath. It also had a restaurant where they served food on longer trips, and there were also comfortable benches and a restroom.

Some chose to stay out on the deck while others waited in the cabin below. There I sat. Brad's friend had been guarding the box with his life, but he finally put it down for a while. I sat at the dining table near the box. I read the words on the lid, and they sunk into my very soul. It all seemed so surreal. I finally touched the box. It wasn't as awful as I had imagined, yet it wasn't my son. I had to get away.

I went to the back of the boat, and it seemed like it took hours to reach our destination. The somber mood was everywhere. I sat on the back deck with my feet up on a railing and just watched the other boats go by. Most were much larger than ours. The wind seemed to blow through me, although it wasn't cold. I just kept waiting, looking down at the water, trying to take everything in . . . this wasn't happening. I felt like soon I'd wake up in my bed and get a call saying Patrick was off the oxygen, getting stronger, and going back to physical therapy.

Suddenly I was startled by the sound of the motor shutting off; it was like waking up from a bad dream. The scary monsters were there, and all the bad things in the dream you dreaded were now all about to come true. The boat came to a sudden stop, as did my heart. Everyone gathered toward the back, where I had been sitting alone. One of my daughters took a video of the ceremony, and I didn't realize until much later while watching the video that Brad and I had both chosen to wear orange shirts that day. Orange had been Patrick's favorite color until it changed to red.

Everyone's faces looked so sad, and mine was so very lost. Brad said a few words then took what was left of his beloved son and gently lowered the bag into the ocean and wiped the tears from his eyes as he said, "I love you, buddy."

We all stood for a moment longer, then everyone seemed to go away. Some went to the front of the boat. The teachers went over to the side in the back, probably to give our family some privacy. The rest went down into the cabin. I just sat there in disbelief.

I'm not sure it really sank in for anyone that day. Since Patrick was in the ICU, most of his friends didn't get a chance to see him or say goodbye; many of his friends had no idea he was even sick since it happened during the summer. As their senior year started, several kids didn't even know where Patrick was or what had happened.

We started again, heading back to shore. For a brief moment of insanity, I wanted to leap into the water and save my son. I was frantic, having a panic attack, and couldn't understand why everyone was just going their own way, leaving Patrick behind as if he didn't matter. It seemed like they could just discard him as a piece of trash to be thrown away and forgotten about. *I needed to get to him!*

I found myself talking to God, saying, "Remember the gift? How can you give me a gift to be able to have more children just to take them away? It's not fair. I want him back! I need him more than you do."

Luckily, my daughter was there, and she said, "But Mom, Patrick isn't there." She was right and I knew it. That wasn't my son. That was what remained of his body. I knew his spirit lived on in a happier place. He was free like a bird now. Had God even taken him anywhere, or was he right there beside me, with us all, watching the entire time? If we could see what we cannot see, then maybe we could finally see.

Even still, at that very moment I needed to grasp onto something—anything—to capture that moment in time, something I felt would give me a piece of him. I needed something tangible that I could touch, feel, and hold on to. Then I saw it. I wasn't quite sure what "it" was, but I grabbed it. It weighed maybe two pounds or less, and I told my daughter, "I'm stealing this; I have to." I put it in my pocket. It was so small that I knew nobody would miss it. After all, this boat was lined with them, whatever "it" was. It was mine, a piece of that moment in time I could hold on to and use to remember my baby boy forever.

When we got to shore, I went into the gift shop and purchased a Galveston Island t-shirt. I don't want to ever ruin it, so I have only worn it once. I also bought a mood necklace that turns green, blue, and purple and has an anchor with a captain's wheel on the front—the same symbol that was on one of Patrick's baby outfits.

As soon as I got back to my hotel room, I called Scott in Salt Lake City and told him that I had stolen something. I couldn't handle the guilt and had to make it right. He asked me what it was. I said, "I don't know." He seemed confused, so I tried to explain it to him, and he figured it out. We had been on what was known as a deep-sea ocean liner used for deep-sea fishing. I had taken a weight that helped the line sink to the bottom of the ocean floor. (Now I understand the term, "Hook, line, and sinker.") Scott said not to worry, that we'd call once I got home and pay for it, find a way to replace it, or send it back.

When I finally got hold of the captain and told her who I was and what I had done, she was so sweet. She told me not to even worry about it. She just wanted the number off of it so she could put another in its place. I still have it and forever will. It sits just above me on my desk where I write.

My friends, everyone from AA, and so many from my church were so generous in helping us get our child buried. It was an expense we just couldn't afford.

For those who have never lost a child, a sibling, or other loved one, grief is a difficult thing. We all react differently. No two people grieve the same, just as no two children are the same. Some get through it rather quickly; for others, it seems to take more time; and I feel for most, it never goes away. You just learn to live differently, without that person in your life. I like to compare it to a family sending a son or daughter off to war. Let's say you don't get to talk to your child at all. After three months, you really miss him. After six months, you miss him even more. Do you think just because a year goes by, you'd miss him any less? Of course not; the longer he is gone, the more you yearn to have him back and the more you miss him—and the harder life becomes living without him.

I believe our loved ones are not far away. They often come to us in different ways to let us know they are okay. I had that experience after the boat took off and everyone left. The gazillion seagulls that swarmed the boat just kept coming back over and over. I was so amazed and regret that I didn't know how to work the video portion on my phone. It was so incredible; I had never seen anything like it, ever. They followed for such a great distance.

It's the simple things that can remind you. I was once at a meeting, and there was a young kid there wearing a black shirt and a bright-red pair of tennis shoes. How many people do you know who own bright-red tennis shoes? I later

learned this kid with the dirty-blonde hair was named Patrick
. . . I was stunned.

Another time we went to a Journey concert in July 2014.
We were sitting on the grass as other bands were playing
before Journey came on. I was missing Patrick and feeling
sad. All of a sudden in front of me someone was passing
through. All I saw was a bright-red pair of tennis shoes that
seemed to be almost in my lap. I quickly glanced up, but
whoever it was had gone. At that very moment, two lone
seagulls flew by. It made me smile.

About nine months after Patrick died, things got real. I
tried several methods of escape—mostly sleeping, as I had
fibromyalgia. I was somewhat suicidal because I wanted to
be with Patrick. I have read stories from other parents who
long to be with their children. We are not crazy or suicidal. I
believe this is just a normal reaction, giving us a glimmer of
hope—if we need to be with a loved one badly enough, we
know we can be.

However, I know that's not the way it really works.
Unfortunately, life includes pain. We all have to lose loved
ones, and we all have to die ourselves. But we will all live
again in Christ, and I know I will be reunited with my Patrick in God's due time. Until then, he'll be an angel on my
shoulder.

CHAPTER THIRTEEN

quit my job at Occurrence when I was no longer able to work from home. My supervisor and I were taking some new calls. I had to go to the bathroom and apparently missed a few when the rush came in. He started yelling at me and belittling me and said I had to come in and work onsite. The tension was building, and I could almost feel Brad hovering over me, catching my every little mistake and scolding me for it. I started to cry as I packed my things to head for the office.

The closer I got to work during my twenty-minute drive, the madder I got. *Screw him*, I thought to myself. *I'm quitting.* I walked in and pretty much told him off. He said it was for missing calls and not getting sales for my supervisor; I just went to the bathroom and wasn't gone very long. My supervisor asked me to take our conversation off the floor where other employees couldn't hear us. I simply left my things there and walked out. I felt so empowered.

I needed and loved my job, but I never could have worked under his eagle's eye watching my every move and listening to my calls. It reminded me too much of Brad hovering over me whenever I was on the computer, so quick to point out

when I was doing something wrong and many times screaming at me for not understanding.

The whole thing, including everything I had experienced
in my life, demonstrates what trauma looks and feels like. In
short, it involves:

- An inability to think of the trauma
- Flashbacks
- Inability to concentrate
- Negative thinking
- Difficulty sleeping
- Feeling guilt or shame
- Negative moods
- Always feeling on guard
- Loss of interest
- Bad dreams

To heal trauma, you have to work with the body, mind,
and spirit. That is why I go to the therapist I do, as she treats
all three.

If you've experienced trauma, these things are not all in
your head—even if a doctor tells you they are, like mine did
in Houston. Trauma can cause all kinds of symptoms in your
body as your cells remember every single experience that's
ever happened to you. Some doctors are just uneducated in
certain areas.

Have you personally ever experienced trauma? Do you
know the symptoms of post-traumatic stress disorder? Many
people have nightmares, feel on edge, experience flashbacks,

keep others at a distance, don't trust others, are never able to fully relax, or are unable to feel comfortable in their own skin. Entire books have been written on the symptoms alone. I often think my trauma has been healed or is gone, but then I find myself screaming as my son or husband comes walking down the stairs to our basement bedroom, even though I know that person is coming and who it is. I just can't help it. I am also isolated and have extreme trust issues.

You could do therapy all day for several years, and talk all day, but if you don't address your body, mind, and spirit, not much will happen. Let me explain why.

The brain functions differently when something traumatic happens to a person. Under normal circumstances, the brain encodes whatever it needs to encode. Every cell in your body remembers every tiny detail of what has happened to you, even if you don't consciously remember it yourself. Things that happen are processed, stored, and then disposed of. This allows life to go on with your memories intact. However, there is a completely different process when someone is under stress.

For us to survive, our bodies are full of all kinds of chemical and electrical impulses that constantly communicate. These impulses tell our brain and body what to do. "Process this, pay a lot of attention to that, don't bother worrying about this, it's not important, this one is very critical to hold to, that one you can discard" . . . and so forth. Under normal circumstances, the only messages you get are the ones that need to be paid attention to—you are fully present, encoding the information, and it's not a big deal. You feel calm and everything seems and feels normal to you.

Any time that we are processing information, we form explicit memories and implicit memories. *Explicit memories* are factual information, general knowledge, and autobiographical information. These are things that we already know. *Implicit memories* are the emotional responses and body sensations. They don't have to do with fact; instead, they involve feeling. Some call it a "knowing," or intuition, among other things. These two types of memories both travel in different pathways in the brain and have to be integrated later to form one unified memory. Have you ever had the feeling of just knowing something without having the ability to explain why?

Under stress, however, everything goes crazy.

In a traumatic situation, your "fight-or-flight" response gets triggered. Your body senses danger and sends out red flags in the form of hormones. Your bloodstream is then swimming with chemical messengers that are telling you to GET OUT NOW! The primary goal under these circumstances isn't encoding the memory but getting you to safety. Its goal is to get you out of harm's way. That is why so many trauma victims have gaps in memory: the attention was focused on getting the body to safety.

I have very few memories of my childhood. It is normal for some adults who have been severely traumatized in childhood to have very little or next to no memory of their childhood. This is the mind's and body's way of protecting them, a way for them to survive as the trauma is too horrific to endure with the natural human mind. It's beyond comprehension. The symptoms of post-traumatic stress, one of which is anxiety, are the same signals that the body sends when you are in danger: your heart beats faster, and your breathing races. Your body wants to shut down the extra impulses like getting oxygen to your muscles. This is why some people seem to freeze when frightened, unable to move, and may hold their breath. Post-traumatic stress also shuts down your hunger or need to use the restroom. Your hands may begin to shake. Your palms become sweaty, and adrenaline fuels your energy so that you can get out. Some people get such a rush of adrenaline they gain superhuman strength.

These are all normal responses to stress. The problem begins when you get stuck. Some people think those of us who get stuck are weak, but we are not. Our bodies just respond to stress differently.

When you get stuck, your amygdala—the part of the brain that is the primary culprit in the fight-or-flight response—gets really sensitive. If you've ever seen a deer in the wild, you've seen the amygdala at work. This part of your brain screams GET OUT when it senses you are in danger. Your brain stops processing and focuses all of its energy on getting you away from danger. The memory doesn't get fully processed at that moment and is fragmented in the brain in pockets of implicit and explicit memories. This is why sometimes a smell, taste, feel, or even the sound or tone of a person's voice can trigger a trauma victim. These can be everyday things that wouldn't normally trigger you had these experiences not happened to you.

It's very important to remember that your body cannot tell the difference between physical and emotional danger. This is the reason you have this fight-or-flight response to stimuli, whether it is emotional or physical. Therein lays a huge danger. The primal part of your brain involved here thinks you are in physical danger, which is why you have the physical symptoms, even when you may be safe from harm of any kind.

To solve the problem, you need to confront the physical head-on. The issue, then, involves a two-part answer. First, you need to bring the body's response down and calm down your hormonal messengers that are telling you that you are in danger, because you are not. Then you will be able to work on the mental and emotional aspects of the problem. You need to have a safe place where you can do this; if you don't do it, you are setting yourself up for failure.

So, the next time that you are struggling with healing from your trauma, remind yourself that your body is doing exactly what it is supposed to do to protect you. Remember that it is acting in a normal manner to an abnormal situation you experienced. You'll need to work on reprogramming your inner navigation alarm system.

A good psychologist or therapist will tell you that walking through the fear head-on is the best and fastest way to overcome it. A good therapist can walk through your journey with you, so you know you are safe and not alone in helping your body understand that you are no longer in danger.

Working together, you can process the trauma so that it is a part of your story and not something that needs avoiding. Remember, you need to feel to heal. You just need to work with your body as well as your mind and spirit, because they are intrinsically interconnected. You cannot work on just one without the others and expect to be successful.

The term used for being present in our bodies is *mindfulness*. There are several mindfulness meditation talks you can listen to. One of my favorites is Headspace. There are other apps for smartphones besides Headspace that will work for you as well. You can begin this process on your own. You can also find several coping mechanisms on the internet; Google them. There are also several ways that you can start to calm your body down. It's a very simple process that can be done virtually anytime and anyplace. Diaphragmatic breathing techniques are wonderful for this because they signal to your body that you're not actually in danger.

Some things to always remember are "Calm" and "Stop, Breathe, Think." It may take a moment to explore different techniques until you find one that is just right for you, but don't give up. Help is out there, and everyone has a program that's right for them, so if one thing doesn't seem to work, don't hesitate to try another to find what's best for you.

Having your memory slip away can also be brought on by PTSD. Stress can add all kinds of things to our bodies that may take on the form of an illness. It can mimic fibromyalgia, chronic fatigue syndrome, and ADHD; it can even actually cause auto-immune diseases. People who are deeply disturbed or have split personalities can even have a change of eye color as they go from one personality to another, and their blood type has even been known to change.

So, do what you can—take a bath, ride your bike, walk along a beautiful trail, sit and watch the sunset while listening to relaxing music, or whatever calms you down when you begin to feel anxious. *Know* you are okay. Let a well-trained therapist who works with mind, body, and spirit help you to heal. It's not all in your head . . . your body remembers more than you'll ever know, and it's ingrained in every cell. You need a healthy body and a clear mind for your spirit to thrive.

Remember to always put yourself first. Just like they tell you when you board an airplane, first put your own oxygen mask on then help the next person. You won't be able to help anyone else if you are not fully prepared and healthy. Eat well, sleep comfortably, and exercise with joy, knowing you have a body that works for you. Even if it's not like everyone else's, it's yours, and you can do amazing things with what you have.

A song entitled "You Say" by Lauren Daigle seems to be talking to the one who matters most—God—and provides powerful reminders for all of us.

- We fight voices in our mind telling us we're not enough and that we'll never measure up. This is what I call the "Fat, Ugly, Stupid syndrome," never feeling good enough. Yet we are way beyond what we know. Those little negative voices are lies.

- We question our self-worth, and in abusive situations, that is ten times worse than the average person with those very same thoughts.
- We need to remember who we really are. We are daughters of a loving Heavenly Father, and we are of infinite worth.
- When we are feeling worthless, we need to remember we are loved so very much. God knows our strengths, even if all we feel are our weaknesses. As long as we do all we can do, we will never fall short; He will always be there to help us on our way. You may not feel you belong or fit in anywhere, but remember who made you and whose you really are.
- It doesn't matter what others think of us; in fact, what other people think of me is none of my business. I'm only here to please God, and what He thinks of me is what matters. He shows me who I really am—my true identity.
- We have to turn our will and life over to the care of a loving God. We need to give Him our failures so He can ease our burdens and thank Him when we rise and are victorious, because it's only through Him that we can truly shine.

Don't settle for anything less than the best. No one deserves to be abused in any form or shape whatsoever. There's just no excuse for abuse!

Remember who you are, where you came from, and where you are going once you leave this earth. Remember your divine nature as a daughter of God, and you will always *know* that you are good enough.

CHAPTER FOURTEEN

The Covid-19 pandemic impacted the world's health and economy in a myriad of ways. But did you know it also caused a spike in the incidence of domestic abuse? Those in quarantine with an abuser suffered surges in domestic violence. I share the following from theguardian.com:

> Cases typically spike in times of economic crisis—and, with most of the US told to stay home, hotlines are worried victims can't leave.
>
> One caller to a domestic violence hotline reported that her husband threatened to throw her out into the street if she coughed. Another reported she had been strangled by her partner but feared going to the hospital because of the threat of coronavirus. An immunocompromised man from Pennsylvania called in after his emotionally abusive girlfriend began hiding cleaning supplies and hand sanitizers from him.

With more than three-quarters of the US told to stay home to stem the pandemic's spread, nowhere is safe for victims of intimate partner violence. A self-quarantine puts them in perpetual proximity to their abuser. Leaving exposes them not just to a deadly virus but a world that has largely closed its doors.

Activists worldwide have reported an alarming rise in domestic violence cases since the start of coronavirus. In Wuhan in February, while the province was under strict lockdown, one police station reported a threefold increase in complaints compared with the same period last year. Advocates are concerned that this bleak reality has reached the United States, where experts say one in four women and one in seven men face physical violence by a partner at some point in their lifetimes.

The National Domestic Violence Hotline, which typically receives up to 2,000 calls per day, counted 951 callers between 10 and 24 March who mentioned Covid-19 while reporting their abuse.

One caller, from New York, reported being awakened from bed because she had a fever and wasn't feeling well. Her abuser threw her out of the front door and kept their child. Another told the hotline she was being kept home against her will after being threatened by her abuser with a hammer and an unregistered gun. He was using the pandemic as an excuse to stop her from leaving him, she said.

"We are hearing from survivors how Covid-19 is already being used by their abusive partners to further control and abuse, how Covid-19 is already impacting their ability to access support and services like accessing shelter, counseling, different things that they would typically lean on in their communities."

As of this writing, we are still supposed to stay at home if at all possible. The only places widely open are those where people can get food, and many grocery stores limit the number of shoppers allowed at a time, since we are also supposed to be practicing social distancing, meaning staying at least six feet from others. We're supposed to be in contact with just our immediate family—no social gatherings. For the first time in history, The church of Jesus Christ of Latter-day Saints closed worldwide to help prevent the spread of Covid-19.

Everywhere you go, you see people wearing masks. We are now being told not to leave home without them. So many people are out of work. Restaurants are closed except for those doing delivery or curbside service. Only essential businesses are open. Americans are filing for unemployment at an alarming rate, and stay-at-home initiatives have been enacted in various places.

I am so glad I am not still married to Brad. I remember going through Hurricane Ike, in which we had no water or electricity for four days. It hit September 13, 2008. At first, everything seemed fine. I did the weekly grocery shopping and had the cart filled to the brim. Then I found out a pair of Latter-day Saint missionaries were going to be staying with us because their apartment was flooded in Pearland, Texas. I decided to go back to the store about an hour later and was shocked to find almost all the shelves were barren. All the fresh dairy and meats were gone; there was no bread; there were just a few tortillas and some canned goods. So much for the extra snacks I planned on getting for the missionaries.

We have now been adding to our food storage powdered milk and lots of drinking water to be more prepared for whatever may be coming. These are uncertain times, and life is anything but normal.

Scott was furloughed from his night job; he still has his day job, but as of this writing, he has been on only two calls. The world seems to have shut down. It's been a challenge being in quarantine with my husband and nineteen-year-old son, Cameron, who are about the only people I see.

Stress is high; add to that economic insecurity. People are taking their own lives, and children are being abused more as well. School used to be their safe place, and that has now been taken away from them. Violence against children reports have gone down—but because they have not been allowed to go to school, no one can report suspected abuse. Seniors in high school will not be going to their prom and also will not be walking for graduation. Most company-related issues are being done online, and groceries are being delivered to homes for people who don't want to go out. Even meals are being delivered from the restaurants that are still open.

How can you cope? Find humor wherever you can to release the stress load. I'm so very grateful I have an elliptical, treadmill, and incline treadmill in my home along with various other portable workout products. I can't imagine how regulars at the gym feel with all gyms being closed. For now, you can walk and bike while practicing social distancing outdoors and getting some exercise.

Many states are on strict lockdown, leaving us all just wondering when things will be getting back to normal and what the new normal will look like. I am praying for all the women and children who are literally stuck at home with no way out.

Update from mid-May: Today, things are slowly opening up again. My husband just went to work today for his night job at the Kearns Fitness Center, where he cleans pools among other things; they will be doing a partial opening next week. More restaurants have opened for dining. Everywhere you go you still see people wearing masks; it's mandatory for employees. Everyone is wondering and waiting for when life will get back to normal or if it ever will at all.

Abuse and domestic violence have only gotten worse. All we can do is educate ourselves and get out of toxic relationships before it is too late.

Update from December 3, 2020: Everyone is excited for this year to end. Covid-19 is still running rampant. Earlier this year, there was an earthquake here in Utah, and there have been disasters around the world. Everyone is calling this the "new normal."

I can correlate that with my life, how it was and how it is now. I am now living the "new normal." I've had almost eleven years of bliss with my new husband. There have been a few bumps in the road and hurdles to overcome, but I am telling you it is possible to find that one who will truly love and respect you. To all women out there still struggling, don't *ever* give up!

In the endearing tale of *Winnie the Pooh*, Christopher Robin muses, "We get to where we are going only by walking away from where we've been."

CONCLUSION

To sum up, I want to offer four tips and warning signs to help you avoid an abusive relationship.

1. **When you are vulnerable, dating is a bad idea. Period.** In war, soldiers must fortify their base before carrying out any other tasks. You too must "fortify your base" if you are feeling vulnerable. Until you have secured your base and found healthy emotional ground, it is not a good idea to date. Not anyone.

2. **Always follow your gut.** With one man, I had a hunch that his kind gestures in the beginning were just an act and that he might really be a psychopath. At the time, I thought this was such a ridiculous assumption that I blew it off. He had done nothing up to that time to prove my hunch correct; little did I know that one day I would be shocked by the accuracy of my gut instinct. Always trust your gut instinct. It is your body's way of protecting you, and it's rarely wrong.

3. **Don't be vulnerable.** I cannot stress enough that you should not bother to date if you are vulnerable. A lot of people will ignore this suggestion because

when you are vulnerable, you often become needy and want to find another person to fill this void. It's a very bad idea. When you feel lonely, seek out friends of the same gender and go do fun things like shopping or getting your hair and nails done—but stay away from men at all costs.

4. **Depend on yourself.** The only person you can truly depend on is yourself. You must cultivate this self-assurance and independence to avoid falling prey to abusive relationships in the future. No one else can save you. If you end up in a relationship in which a white knight proclaims he will take all your tears away, brace yourself. Often when we allow these types of people in our lives, we give away our power without even realizing it.

Falling prey to an abuser has nothing to do with your intelligence. Do not let anyone make you feel stupid for ending up in an abusive situation. Vulnerability and self-esteem issues that often stem from childhood are common reasons people fall into these relationships. Even after leaving an abusive relationship, until you can understand more about your weaknesses and fortify your base, you might still fall prey to abusers. That is why we tend to pick the same kind of men over and over until we learn to rely on and trust ourselves. Counseling is one indispensable tool that can help you build your self-worth and cultivate ways to avoid falling prey to abusive relationships and unhealthy friendships in your future.

If you or someone you know is trapped in an abusive relationship and needs help, you can call The National Domestic Violence Hotline. It is open twenty-four hours a day.

After all this, what about me and my family?

Brooke, my oldest daughter, is doing well, as is her boyfriend. She was just put on disability for PTSD and knows she is an alcoholic. I just hope she does what is necessary before she loses her choice to do so if it's not already too late. She did not speak to me for about six years; I don't know why. Once when I left Brad, she got really mad. When I came back to him, she got even madder. She seems to get along okay with him now and says she has just dealt with the past and gotten through it. She and I get along very well today.

I have not heard from my second-oldest daughter, Jessica, for about two and a half years. I know she drinks a lot. When we do talk, which is usually by text, there is nothing I can say that she doesn't take personally; she ends up cursing and bashing me horribly with her words, making me feel like I've done something terribly wrong. I have to let my husband read the messages to make double sure that I was being very sensitive to her emotions and didn't say anything that could have upset her, but somehow, she finds a way to pick out something. It's sad, because she and I used to be so close. Now she stays pretty much to herself, and no one knows exactly where she lives.

My oldest son, Zach, has a severe social anxiety disorder, but he says he's learned to manage it, and we get along great.

He's had a good job at the front desk at Best Western Hotel for several years now.

My youngest daughter, Dani, and I get along well most of the time, but she and I can butt heads like no other. I don't like her husband; he is a heroin addict and was even using this past summer while they were staying here. I can't count how many times he supposedly lost her phone or left it on the bus, when he probably sold it to buy drugs, and he is constantly belittling her while she is the one working full time and bringing home all the money so they can survive. One of his friends lives with him as a roommate and helps with the bills.

My youngest son, Cameron, is almost twenty and still living at home. He's high-functioning autistic. We've been working on him getting his driver's license for a while, but he keeps failing the tests. They recently gave his expired permit a six-month extension due to the Covid-19. He had a job interview at Chick-Fil-A, but the Coronavirus messed that up too; they stopped hiring since they are only doing drive-through.

Finally, my husband and I are getting along great!

ABOUT THE AUTHOR

Malia grew up with an alcoholic father, a neurotic mother, and a troubled brother in the Los Angeles area, where she was born. She endured many hardships involving abuse, tragedy, and a life no child should *ever* have to live. Through one trauma after another, she made her way through life holding on to the one thing she knew was certain—God's hand.

She often wondered if God was really there; her bad life just kept getting worse, until she remembered its beginnings, which she had blocked out for so many years. She now puts those horrible experiences in the back corners of her mind and refuses to let her horrendous past define the woman she is today.

Malia is proof that with God's help, you can get through anything.

Malia resides in Utah with her loving husband and their two youngest children. Although she struggles with insecurities and sometimes doubts herself, she pushes forward, truly believing she is a child of God and therefore of infinite worth and value. She knows that bad things can happen to good people, as they did to her, but they don't make someone bad. With all of her past behind her, she is happy today, and her life just keeps getting better as she follows God's plan for her.

For several years, Malia has dreamed of visiting the Virgin Islands. Once all the Covid-19 restrictions have lifted, she and Scott plan on going to one of the islands there and discovering paradise on earth.

A free ebook edition is available with the purchase of this book.

To claim your free ebook edition:

1. Visit MorganJamesBOGO.com
2. Sign your name CLEARLY in the space
3. Complete the form and submit a photo of the entire copyright page
4. You or your friend can download the ebook to your preferred device

Morgan James
BOGO™

A FREE ebook edition is available for you
or a friend with the purchase of this print book.

CLEARLY SIGN YOUR NAME ABOVE

Instructions to claim your free ebook edition:
1. Visit MorganJamesBOGO.com
2. Sign your name CLEARLY in the space above
3. Complete the form and submit a photo
   of this entire page
4. You or your friend can download the ebook
   to your preferred device

Print & Digital Together Forever.

Snap a photo

Free ebook

Read anywhere

CPSIA information can be obtained
at www.ICGtesting.com
Printed in the USA
JSHW031922140122
22027JS00003B/3